D1251366

Changing Aims in Economics

JB

Changing Aims in Economics

TERENCE HUTCHISON

BLACKWELL
Oxford UK & Cambridge USA

The right of Terence Hutchison to be identified as author of this
work has been asserted in accordance with the Copyright,
Designs and Patents Act 1988.
First published 1992

Blackwell Publishers
108 Cowley Road
Oxford OX4 1JF
UK

Three Cambridge Center
Cambridge, Massachusetts 02142
USA

British Library Cataloguing in Publication Data
A CIP catalogue record for this book is available from the British
Library.

Library of Congress Cataloging-in-Publication Data
Hutchison, T. W. (Terence Wilmot)
Changing Aims in Economics / Terence Hutchison.
p. cm.
Includes bibliographical references and index.
ISBN 0–631–18498–8
1. Economics – History – 20th century. 2. Economic policy.
I. Title
HB87.H88 1992
330 – dc20 91–38301 CIP

Typeset in 12 on 14 pt Garamond
by Graphicraft Typesetters Ltd., Hong Kong
Printed in Great Britain by Billings Ltd., Worcester

'The most important part of education – to teach the meaning of to know (in the scientific sense).'

Simone Weil
(The last sentence in her notebook)

The 'Professor Dr. P. Hennipman Stichting' was founded at the initiative of the 'Kring van Amsterdamse Economen' (Circle of Amsterdam Economists) on the occasion of Professor Hennipman's retirement from his Chair in the Faculty of Economics at the University of Amsterdam. The Foundation is administered by a Board of Dutch economists who are, for the greater part, university professors.

P. Hennipman served the Amsterdam Faculty from 1938 until 1974, covering a broad field of subjects in economic theory in his brilliant and very thorough lectures. In this way, he trained and inspired many generations of students, and equipped them with analytical tools and scientific practices of inestimable value in their careers in science, education, business and politics. Like his lectures, Hennipman's publications are characterized by his almost unique way of carefully and profoundly weighing all aspects of the subject, based on sharp-witted thinking and reasoning, combined with linquistic refinements on the one hand, and on an encyclopaedic knowledge of relevant literature on the other.

In honour of P. Hennipman, the Foundation has undertaken to organize, every two years, a lecture by an outstanding economist, and these lectures will be published in an elaborated form as monographs. Fortunately, it has been possible to co-ordinate this goal with the activities of the Professor F. de Vries Foundation, and as a result, lectures will be published annually under the alternate auspices of the two Foundations in a combined series entitled 'Lectures in Economics-Theory, Institutions, Policy'.

Contents

[vii]

Preface

I wish first to express my thanks for having been invited to contribute to the Hennipman Lectures, named after such a great scholar and such a distinguished writer on the methodology of economics. For me, this subject has been a main interest since I first began to study economics in the early 1930s, in the middle of the great depression. I regard the principal aim of methodological writing and criticism to be the achieving of more clarity, and less obscurity and confusion, regarding, on the one hand, the inadequacies and limitations of economic knowledge, and on the other, its progress, such as it has been, and its possibilities. If exaggerated public hopes and subsequent dangerous disillusion are to be avoided, a saving degree of clarity and realism regarding these questions about economic knowledge and ignorance should be considered not only as of academic or philosophical interest but as highly desirable among the wider circle of students of economics at all levels, as well as among those concerned with economic policy-making. In this lecture another attempt is made to illustrate that more progress in achieving this kind of clarity, and in reducing this kind of obscurity and confusion, is as important as ever.

The lecture was delivered in Amsterdam in September 1990. For publication I was required to undertake a large expansion of the original, oral version. This expansion has been made partly in the text but in large measure in the notes. I hope that anyone who takes the trouble to read the text will also read the notes, in which it has been possible to include, as also in the 'Postscript', references to some controversial items from the flood of recent (1990–1) contributions to the issues discussed in this lecture. The increasing intensity in the last year or two, of the discussion of fundamental methodological and educational issues, by a wide variety of economists, seems, to this writer, not to have been equalled at any time in the six decades through most of which he has been more or less concerned with such questions. There is a very great deal to be clarified, and, if possible, resolved. Indeed, for quite a number of economists, this last decade of the century probably should be, and, just conceivably might be, the methodological decade.

I very much regret that, these days, notes have to be separated from the text, instead of appearing at the foot of the page. It has recently been suggested by Dr Gertrude Himmelfarb (in the *New York Times Book Review*, 16 June 1991, p. 1) that, as a consequence of the separation of notes from text, less care is being taken to ensure the accuracy of references. I can only hope that no serious diminution in accuracy occurs here. It does seem to me, however, that now notes are at some distance from the text, and, presumably, are not so often read concurrently, their potentially interesting discursive function (as contrasted with their referential or bibliographical function) may be indulged in rather more freely, with less danger of such additional appendages so frequently holding up, or distracting from, the main line of argument – especially in the case of a work as brief as this.

I am very grateful to Roger Backhouse for reading an earlier version of the typescript and for his valuable comments and suggestions, and also for providing me with copies of a number of important recent articles, including his own. I also wish to thank Denis O'Brien for some valuable suggestions. Finally, I would like to record my deep debt of gratitude to my wife for helping me to remove many stylistic and grammatical errors and infelicities and for her constant encouragement and support.

T. W. H.

1

From Petty to Keynes

Sir William Petty has been recognized from extremely differing points of view (as far apart, for example, as those of Karl Marx and Friedrich Hayek) as a, or the, founding father of modern political economy. The particular viewpoint from which I would emphasize Petty's founding role is a methodological one: Petty undertook the first serious attempt to establish our subject on 'scientific', or would-be 'scientific', foundations. What distinguished Petty from his 'mercantilist' predecessors and contemporaries did not relate to the overriding objective (which they shared) of providing guidance for policy. What originated with Petty was the aim or attempt to base economic policies on rather more reliable, intellectually disciplined foundations, or methods, with the objective of achieving less unsuccessful and less sectionally biased policies, together with less politically divisive disagreements, and more of a consensus, regarding the policies to be pursued. Petty maintained that the empirical methods, which were then, in the natural sciences, beginning to produce the strikingly rapid and practically fruitful results achieved by his co-founders of the Royal Society of London for the Improvement of Natural Knowledge (1662), were also applicable to the problems of political economy. Many economists today, of course, would find Petty's views naïve and over-optimistic. Certainly also, since Petty's day, the precise formulation of the 'scientific' or 'disciplined' principles, on the basis of which the study of political economy and economics should proceed, has been long and profoundly disputed. Nevertheless, following up, as far as they would go, the methods which were being so successfully employed in some of the natural sciences in the second half of the seventeenth century, may have provided a vital impetus for a significant initial advance, as notably with regard to the basic subject of demography. The work of Petty (1623–87) and of John Graunt (1620–74), with whom Petty was closely associated, together with the slightly later work of Edmund Halley (1656–1742), prepared the way for subsequent, reasonably reliable series of population estimates necessary for reducing the inaccuracy of many kinds of economic and social predictions, which predictions in turn were essential for many less unsuccessful social and economic policies. For example, the investigations of mortality rates and ages provided the basis for life insurance. In the twentieth century, we have, of course, become well aware of the limitations and dangers of applying too far and too rigidly to social and human studies the kinds of methods and criteria developed by the natural sciences. Perhaps, in fact, an even greater danger today comes from the kind of obscurantism which rejects virtually any and every trace of the discipline and criteria associated with the natural sciences.

It was, in any case, certainly believed by the leading writers on political economy in the eighteenth and nineteenth centuries that the kind of 'scientific', or 'disciplined', methodological principles, as applied, for example in medical science, were applicable, and should be applied, *mutatis mutandis*, or as far as was feasible, in political economy, the prime, overriding objective of which was the improvement of the economic condition of humanity, just as the overriding objective of medical science was the improvement of the health of humanity. Almost without exception, the great pre-classical, classical, and neo-classical writers, such as Petty, Boisguilbert, and Locke, through Hume, Steuart, Smith, Quesnay, and Turgot, to Malthus, Ricardo,[1] and J. S. Mill, and down to Marshall, Walras, Wicksell, and Keynes, were immediately, or almost immediately, concerned with the guidance of policy and with policy relevance, with a view to promoting more successful economic policies. The distinction was for some time employed between the 'science' and the 'art' of political economy, with the 'science' regarded as the foundation, or essential prerequisite, for the 'art'.

The objective of the political economist was not

understood simply or narrowly as the production of memoranda or recommendations for cabinet ministers, bank chairmen, or top 'decision-makers'. As the political environment became more democratic, a wider understanding of economic problems among the electorate became an important objective – for John Stuart Mill, for example, in his *Principles*, culminating in its Book V on the role of government. It might be added that a significant aspect of this wider understanding of political economy was the promotion, in the first instance among economists, of a clearer recognition of the limits and limitations of economic knowledge, and of the practical possibilities of its advance – a specialist area in which methodological clarification, and even the history of economic thought, have a part to play.[2]

In listing some of the great economists, from Petty onwards, who would, as a matter of course, often with little or no explicit discussion, have regarded the guidance of policy, or the enlightenment of policy decisions, as the overriding objective of their subject, I ended with Keynes. For, from about the time of his death, just after the Second World War (which might be taken as symbolic of the ending of an era) profound changes gradually gathered momentum with regard to the traditional aims and claims of the subject and the prime position therein of policy enlightenment and policy relevance. In due course this shift was to be accompanied by a markedly diminishing consensus regarding methodological principles. In the last three or four decades, down to 1990, these changes have amounted to a profound shift in 300-year-old attitudes regarding the objectives of the subject, perhaps not accurately describable as a comprehensive 'revolution', but as a transformation which has involved a prominent and well-publicized section of the economics profession. For a long time, down to about 1970, this change met with little or no explicit challenge.

2
The Neo-classicals and Real-world Problems

It might well be maintained that some significant shift and blurring of the overriding objectives of political economy and economics could be traced to around 1870 and the onset of the neo-classical era, when the subject was moving increasingly into the universities. Academic values, criteria, and objectives began gradually to supplement, or even diminish, the dominant position of policy enlightenment and policy relevance. For most of the 100 years or so, however, down to the end of the Second World War, the traditional objective of the subject retained a prime position, largely unchallenged. Certainly most of the leading first- or second-generation neo-classicals, such as, in the UK, Jevons and Marshall, continued to stress, just as or sometimes even more strongly than their classical predecessors, policy relevance and ultimate social improvement as the supreme objective. In Marshall's *Principles* it is laid down: 'The dominant aim of economics in the present generation is to contribute to a solution of social problems' (1961, vol. I, p. 42). (Marshall added, however, that 'a later generation may have more abundant leisure than we for researches that throw light on obscure points in abstract speculation'.)[1]

A. C. Pigou, Marshall's favourite pupil and successor in Cambridge, expressed, certainly in his earlier writings, the most ardent enthusiasm for the practical, 'fruit-bearing' objective of economics. He rejected the idea of knowledge for its own sake as an objective worth pursuing in economics, and did not 'judge that a knowledge of the implications of the type that pure economics can provide has, in and for itself, any large value' (1922, p. 459). Pigou went further: 'Even a thoroughly realistic economic science would not, in and for itself, make any great appeal to me. Practical usefulness, not necessarily, of course, immediate and direct, but still practical usefulness of some sort, is what I look for from this particular department of knowledge' (p. 461).[2] It should be noted, however, that in his later years (as economists tend to do, if and when they mature intellectually) Pigou came to express profound and possibly even somewhat exaggerated scepticism regarding the political process, via which, he had hoped, social improvement might emerge from the application of economic knowledge to policy.

It would certainly be quite incorrect to suggest that the emphasis on policy relevance was confined to British economists. In the USA, as Professor William Parker has observed: 'two intellectual traditions, of British political economy and German historical economics, created American academic economics'. In both of these traditions, though in different ways, policy relevance was seen as a prime objective, which, moreover, as Parker adds, 'fitted well with the empirical and pragmatic bent of American philosophy' (1986, p. 3). As regards other European traditions, those who know only his *Elements of Pure Economics* may not realize that this volume of Léon Walras was originally intended simply as the first of a three-part treatise, which covered, in the second and third volumes, 'Applied Economics' and 'Social Economics', for which the 'Pure Economics' was to serve as an introductory foundation.[3] Furthermore, even, or especially, those who rejected the narrow scope and mainly deductive methods of most of the English classicals and neo-classicals, such as the leading German historical economist Gustav Schmoller, saw the prime objective of the subject, like his Cameralist predecessors, as the provision of guidance and training for administrators and policy-makers (see Balabkins, 1988, ch. 5, pp. 53ff.).

The criticism, however, contains much validity that towards the end of the nineteenth century the leading neo-classicals concentrated too much on refining their abstract analysis of self-adjusting, competitive processes, and paid insufficient attention to the real-world problems of concern to society and policy-makers. The great real-world problem which was long unduly neglected by neo-classical orthodoxy was that of aggregate instability, cyclical

[8]

fluctuations and unemployment. This was the problem which bore most heavily on the poorer classes (most of whom, in the UK, only got the vote after 1884). Most of the early neo-classicals followed their best-known classical predecessors in tending to regard crises and unemployment (perhaps much less unjustifiably in the nineteenth century than in the twentieth) as anomalous, temporary frictions, or 'abnormal' exceptions to a predominantly self-adjusting system. In the UK, apart from the great contribution of Jevons, the subject of aggregate fluctuations and unemployment only began to be taken up at the academic level in the years just before the First World War. There was no British equivalent of Clement Juglar, the French doctor whose great historical and statistical treatise (1862 and 1889) opened up the problems of the trade cycle.

It was only just before the First World War, and, after its vast institutional upheavals, in the 1920s, immediately before the onset of the most profoundly disastrous world slump in modern history, that the subjects of cyclical instability and serious unemployment became a leading concern of many academic economists. This inattention turned out to be woefully belated, for by 1930–2, when the most devastating deflation hit most of the developed world (the only years in this century when Marx's main historical prediction regarding advanced 'capitalism' fleetingly took on any plausibility) the economics 'profession' could produce nothing like a consensus regarding appropriate countermeasures.

[9]

In fact, some economists influential in central Europe opposed any measures, monetary or fiscal, which might have mitigated the utterly lethal deflation.[4] The result, of course, in the then politically most unstable country in Western Europe, was the Hitler regime, the Second World War, and all the accompaniments thereof. At no juncture in modern politico-economic history, or, at any rate, in this century, has the inadequacy of economic knowledge, and the absence of any saving modicum of consensus regarding a profoundly serious economic problem, had more utterly disastrous consequences for the Western or North Atlantic world.[5] If Jevons's lead, half a century previously, had been more widely supported in the ensuing decades, and if, especially, more concern had been shown for compiling basic empirical material, in the form of relevant statistical series, then, though a serious slump would not, presumably, have been averted in 1929–33, some of the intense severity and appalling consequences might, perhaps or probably, have been significantly mitigated. Instead, too many of the neo-classicals had been concentrating too exclusively on abstract deductive analysis, then described as 'pure theory', based on a minimal empirical foundation, or, even, when conceived a prioristically, on virtually no empirical foundation at all.

The great achievement of the neo-classicals was the working-out of the implications of individual demand, choice, utility, and preference, for the allocation of resources. The dogmatic neglect of these underlying neo-classical principles by Marxist economic theorists was to bear a fundamental responsibility for the total and ignominious collapse (60 years after the most serious, but by no means fatal, 'capitalist' crisis) of the Marxist–Communist economies. The most serious charge, however, against the neo-classicals remains the disastrous disarray of the 'profession' generally – apart from one or two famous exceptions – when confronted by the most appallingly consequential politico-economic crisis of this century, at any rate for the more 'advanced' Western countries.

3

Transformation after 1945: the Formalist 'Revolution'

In the 1930s, the creation of 'macro-economics', as a response to the great policy problem of the time, ensured the retention by policy relevance of what had been its traditional position, at least since Sir William Petty, as the overriding objective, motive, or criterion for the work of economists. This objective continued to hold such a position through the Second World War and for some years after. At the same time the development of macro-economics fostered a more empirical approach than had the deductive abstractions of micro-economic analysis or 'pure theory'. In fact the emergence of macro-economics, followed by the requirements of war-time economic management, produced an important increase in statistical material, which in the UK had been notably defective.

Both in the UK and in the USA, following the disasters of the early 1930s, economics may be said to have had a good war, and the subject emerged in 1945 with enhanced prestige and credibility. As Professor Craufurd Goodwin has observed regarding the USA: 'The experience of the 1940s served to confirm by and large the conclusion that the social sciences, and especially economics, had reached the point where they would be directly beneficial to mankind.' After the war, 'economists were credited with helping to avoid the return of economic depression and with constructing a new international economic order' (1989, p. 160).

Professor Goodwin, however, having emphasized the perhaps excessively and naïvely high hopes which American opinion, as represented by some of the big foundations, entertained regarding the potential of economics for providing the basis for less unsuccessful policy-making, goes on to point out how soon disillusion began to set in, so that 'a marriage that seemed made in heaven', between academic economics and some of the major sources of research funds, ended in early divorce. It appeared that economists generally, or in too many cases, were retreating into abstractions. It never seemed (at any rate to officers of the Ford Foundation) 'that the economics profession as a whole had given up its "Ricardian vice"' – a vice to which undisciplined abstractionists are peculiarly liable (p. 166).

For 20–25 years, however, after 1945, for whatever complex reasons, the economies of all, or nearly all, the more advanced countries enjoyed a period of considerable success, especially as compared with the disasters and distress of the 1930s.

[13]

Very high levels of employment were accompanied by only comparatively mild inflation, while, at the same time, in some of the more important countries, almost unprecedentedly high rates of growth were achieved. For all this apparent economic success economists were mostly quite prepared to claim and receive an important share of the credit. At such a juncture fundamental methodological criticism was hardly likely to find a wide audience. By the late 1960s, however, this period of considerable policy success was coming to an end. At the same time new cohorts of graduate students and junior teaching staff in economics departments had been moving through the academic pipelines, acquiring in the process, it appears, some new ideas about the objectives of the subject.

4

Mounting Criticism: 1970–1990

A very remarkable feature of the change which,
since around the middle of the century, has gradually been taking place in the objectives of economists, has been its almost completely inexplicit
character. Far from any manifesto of the new
movement having appeared proclaiming the need
for, or fruitfulness of, greater and more extensive
abstraction, and the desirability of some kind of
pure knowledge for its own sake, there has been
little or nothing in the way of explanation or justification, even in the face of severe criticisms of
excessive abstraction by eminent economists of
different schools and views. Such a reluctance to
explain or defend a case may, perhaps, suggest
a kind of intellectual weakness. There has been
some discussion of the uses and abuses of mathematics in economics, but it is not the employment
of mathematics *per se* with which we are concerned.[1] Though the much more extensive use of

[15]

mathematics certainly facilitated and, to some extent, concealed, the change in objectives, it did not necessitate any such change.

The main evidence, therefore, for the transformation in objectives cannot be found in positive pronouncements but rather in the eventual emergence of serious, fundamental negative criticisms. That some profound change had been taking place may only have become widely recognized around 1970, when with new, pressing real-world problems emerging, a number of vigorous and authoritative views were expressed regarding the extent to which the original objectives of modern political economy were being abandoned. These criticisms were also directed at changes in the methods and education of economists which seemed to be promoting, or assuming, a fundamental change in objectives. The attacks came not from mavericks, methodologists, or outsiders of one stripe or another, but from Nobel laureates, and, in the UK, from leading officers of important teaching and research institutions.

We may begin, however, with what was not quite the first to appear of the criticisms we shall quote, but with a book which gave much the fullest and most systematic account of the new development with which we are here concerned. This book was Benjamin Ward's *What's Wrong with Economics?*, which appeared in 1972 (and which I wish I had read some 18 years before I did). Ward complained of the tendency for abstract mathematical analysis in economics 'to proliferate wildly beyond the ability of anyone to vouch for its connection with the real world' (1972, p. 39). He maintained that a 'revolution' had taken place, one 'that is more profound than the Keynesian', which 'might be called the formalist revolution' (p. 40). Though 'more profound than the Keynesian', this revolution 'was essentially methodological rather than substantive . . . there just are not any fundamental substantive changes of direction brought about' by this new revolution (p. 43). Ward claimed that more than half the leaders of this revolution had been educated in Europe, but did not name names. He then remarked that 'the formalist revolution' was 'virtually without a historian' (p. 243), a situation which is far from being satisfactorily remedied nearly 20 years later. Already in 1972 Ward was insisting on 'the substantial failure' of the formalist revolution. In emphasizing, however, the role of what he called 'story-telling' in economics, Ward conceded that 'formalism' had provided a 'pressure towards systematic story-telling', and towards 'the goal-oriented collection of facts' (p. 188). He concluded, however, that: 'The lesson of economics is that it is not always enough that, for example, practitioners are in substantial agreement as to the properties of acceptable puzzles and their solutions to insure that a science is seriously engaged in the attempt to understand the relevant natural phenomena' (p. 255).

We continue now with other, briefer criticisms, dating from 1970 onwards, which we have grouped under three headings.[2]

First, there has been the charge of *excessive and arbitrary abstraction* and the disregard of reality.

[17]

In his presidential address to the American Economic Association (1970), the Nobel laureate, Wassily Leontief, complained of 'continued preoccupation with imaginary, hypothetical, rather than with observable reality . . . . In no other field of empirical inquiry has so massive and sophisticated a statistical machinery been used with such indifferent results' (1971, pp. 1–3). Ragnar Frisch, another Nobel laureate, condemned what he described as the widespread practice of 'playometrics': 'We should not mobilize an army of people to produce queer assumptions, so to speak on the conveyer band, and deduce consequences from these assumptions. . . . Such exercises may be an entertaining intellectual game . . . . But it might be a dangerous game both socially and scientifically' (1970, p. 163). Frisch was scathing regarding the contribution to real-world problems of economic growth forthcoming from such, then fashionable, devices as the turnpike problem and the analysis of intrinsic paths: 'I feel that the relevance of this type of theorem for active and realistic work on economic development, in industrialized or underdeveloped countries is practically nil' (p. 162). Mr G. D. N. Worswick, then Director of the National Institute of Economic and Social Research, maintained:

> There now exist whole branches of abstract economic theory which have no links with concrete facts and are almost indistinguishable from pure mathematics. Indeed, it might be more correct to say that there have come into being new branches of mathematics whose distinguishing feature is that

some of the axioms and some of the terminology
show traces of the ancestry of this particular branch
of mathematics, which originated in the distant past
in some real economic question (1972, p. 78).[3]

Almost no notice, of course, was taken of such
complaints, but by the end of the 1980s a note of
despair had, in some circles, crept in regarding the
flight from reality. Professor Robert Clower complained: 'Much of economics is so far removed from
anything that remotely resembles the real world that
it's often difficult for economists to take their own
subject seriously' (1989, p. 23). The editor of the
volume in which Clower's complaint occurred
(Professor David C. Colander) remarked that 'for
many economists economic research has become
the art of devising clever models and in doing
so demonstrating one's technical virtuosity' (1989,
p. 33).

A second line of criticism has been concerned
with emphasizing *the break with the past*. It was
noted by Mr Worswick:

All the great economists of the past have been
reformers and there are few contemporary economists who would not claim that their work and
their ideas are intended to contribute in some
degree, however indirectly, to the improvement of
a firm, an industry, a national economy or the world
as a whole. And if it is said that some do not claim
this, there are very few who explicitly proclaim the
uselessness of their work, with the vigour which
G. H. Hardy once attempted to justify pure mathematics (1972, p. 75).

[19]

Similarly, 14 years later, Professor William Parker was emphasizing the same point as Worswick: 'Every one of these great figures from the pre-Smithian mercantilists through Keynes was concerned centrally with the problems of social welfare, as exhibited in major policy concerns of the day' (1986, p. 2). In the development of economics in the USA, Parker observed, 'the emphasis was on a study which, by laying bare "economic principles", served as a guide to policy', that is down to about 1950, when this emphasis was beginning to decline significantly.

A third line of criticism was concerned with *the irrelevance and unsuitability of much university education in economics for work in government and business*, because of the heavily increasing bias towards excessive abstraction. Sir Henry Phelps Brown (1972) maintained:

It may even be that training in advanced economics is actively unhelpful. I find it a common experience that when graduates in economics first assume practical responsibilities they have something to unlearn. One lecturer in economics, latterly much concerned with international aid, has written to me, 'I find I've learnt a good deal in these last years – particularly how misleading most of my economic training has been. Apart from the basic tools of the trade, I find more and more that I draw on economic history rather than anything in development theory.' An academically distinguished economist who has long experience in government service has told me, 'By far the best preparation for

[20]

a useful career in economics *after* the university, is to go to an organization working on practical problems, partly so as to understand how little use a great many of the academic gadgets are' (1972, p. 2).

At the same time Mr Worswick was warning (1972):

The danger is that university courses in economics will become increasingly mathematical and increasingly concerned with technique to the exclusion of the subject matter itself. Such an imbalance is perhaps less dangerous for students going on to be professional economists than for those going on to posts in business or government . . . those going into government and business, finding such a large gap between what they have learned and the realities with which they are now confronted, may be inclined to dismiss all, and not merely some of what they have learned as of no conceivable relevance to their future work (1972, p. 84).

Previously Professor W. R. Allen had made a similar point when he quoted distinguished government economists in the USA as stating:

The economic theory we are using is the theory most of us learned as sophomores . . . . I think the economists' framework is the right one to weigh the advantages and disadvantages as best you can see them – but when economists sit down and prepare models to try to trace out these consequences in any sophisticated fashion, I think it's just about as apt to be misleading as it is to be

[21]

helpful' (1974, pp. 13–14; quoted by Hutchison, 1977, p. 169).

More recently Sir Alec Cairncross concluded as follows about the uselessness of the more refined economic 'theory' for real-world economists in government:

> I never saw much use made of the more refined and esoteric parts of economic theory. I concluded, as my colleague, the late Ely Devons put it, that 'in so far as economic theory is useful in enabling us to understand the real world and in helping us to take decisions on policy, it is the simple, most elementary and, in some ways, the most obvious propositions that matter' (Cairncross, 1986, p. 3; Devons, 1961, pp. 13–14).

Regarding graduate education in the USA, William Parker has complained (1986) that 'in graduate programs over the past 25 years, theory has come to be elevated to a central place while being itself more and more narrowly and rigorously defined' (p. 7). Parker continued:

> The institutional content, the social concepts, the moral zeal implicit in the training which economists used to be given through courses in economic history, economic institutions and applied fields have been pushed aside while these fields have themselves been partially transformed or distorted into playgrounds for the imagination of the theorist (p. 7).

Before returning to the subject of graduate education in economics in the USA we may note briefly

[22]

a criticism about the waste involved in excessively abstract economic research in universities, and a remarkable proposal for intervention to counteract this waste. Professor Gordon Tullock has maintained that 'at the moment, economic research is very heavily dominated by non-applied activity' (1989, p. 246). He proposes that a fund of $50m., administered by politicians and businessmen, should be devoted to awards for applied economic research. Tullock explains his objective as the provision of countervailing incentives to overcome what he describes as *the strong social pressures that now exist within the university for abstract and fashionable research* (italics added, 1989, p. 247). Tullock explains: 'I would assume that if my recommendations are followed, a great deal of money would be wasted on projects that seem sensible to politicians, although most economists know that they are pointless. I suggest, however, that this waste would be less than the waste in our present research' (p. 247). Those who appreciate Professor Tullock's capacity for dead-pan humour, as well as profound principled aversion to intervention in (what might be regarded as) free intellectual processes, may wish to reread carefully this proposal before deciding that it does indeed represent a desperate attempt to counter the effects of a seriously antisocial intellectual monopoly.

The criticisms we have been summarizing of economic education in both the USA and the UK, by both American and British economists, have been elaborated and may, on some points, have been confirmed, by some fascinating research surveying the views of graduate students of economics at six well-known American institutions: the universities of Chicago, Columbia, Harvard, Stanford, and Yale, plus the Massachusetts Institute of Technology. The authors of this enterprising and courageous pioneer investigation, Professors Arjo Klamer and David Colander, claim that 'our study of graduate education provides some data in assessing such views as that "departments of economics are graduating a generation of *idiots savants* brilliant at esoteric mathematics yet innocent of actual economic life"' (1990, p. 95).[4] Here we can only quote very briefly from some of the more striking conclusions, while expressing the hope that further surveys of this field will make more evidence available. Summarizing the replies from 212 students in 1985, Colander and Klamer emphasized the following points:

1 'There was a strong sense that economics was a game and that hard work in devising relevant models that demonstrated a deep understanding of institutions would have a lower pay-off than devising models that were analytically neat; the facade, not the depth of knowledge was important' (p. 100).

2 As regards what qualifications would be likely to 'place students on a fast track', or 'make an economist successful', it was found that '68 per cent believed that a thorough knowledge of the economy was unimportant', and only 3.4 per cent thought it

was 'very important' (p. 99); 43 per cent believed that a knowledge of the literature was 'unimportant'.

3   The survey showed that 'graduate students are initially interested in policy. Most entered economics because they hoped it would shed light on policy' (p. 107). The likely reason for students' transformation into technique-oriented individuals on moving from their first-degree colleges into graduate schools is that most of them aspire to academic jobs:[5]

> They know that tenure depends on publication in the right journals. They logically choose a course of study that is most likely to lead to their goal of succeeding in that intermediate goal. Knowing a technique that can be applied to ten areas can lead to ten articles; knowing a specific area well might lead to one or two articles (p. 109).

4   The surveyors observed that 'what students believe leads to success in graduate schools is definitely techniques; success has little to do with understanding the economy, nor has it much to do with economic literature' (p. 109). Colander and Klamer maintain that

> the graduates are well-trained in problem-solving, but it is technical problem-solving which has more to do with formal modeling techniques that with real-world problems. To do the problems little real-world knowledge of institutions is needed, and in many cases such knowledge would actually be a hindrance since the simplifying assumptions would be harder to accept (p. 108).

[25]

These conclusions show a considerable corre-
spondence with the views of the English authorities, Phelps Brown and Worswick, quoted above,
which date from about 15 years earlier. Worswick
had then complained of the element of pretence in
the work of some econometricians: 'They are not,
it seems to me, engaged in forging tools to arrange
and measure actual facts so much as making a
marvelous array of pretend-tools which would per-
form wonders if ever a set of facts should turn up
in the right form' (1972, p. 79).

According to the survey by Klamer and Colander, what appears to have been happening in some
leading American graduate schools is that interest
in real-world policy applications is being drained,
or trained, out of aspiring students of economics,
which, at the graduate-school level, is becoming a
subject which is taught to graduate students to a
large extent so that these graduate students, or the
more 'successful' of them, may, in turn, go on to
teach it to succeeding cohorts of graduate students,
with a minimum impingement, at any point, on or
from the real world outside the graduate institutions.
At one time this charge used to be brought against
the then extensive university teaching of the ancient languages – a charge which possessed, one
might venture to suggest, very much less educational justification. Recently, in fact, it has been
claimed as part of the sales pitch of an economics
department in the UK that 'studying economic theory
is a means of developing the mind which is one

of the purposes of higher education' (Sloane, 1990, p. 20). It might be suggested that if students are simply seeking a training of the mind then they should more suitably study the ancient classical languages or pure mathematics, where the dangers of misunderstandings as to the relevance of what they are studying for contemporary real-world problems, would not be so serious. Incidentally, Klamer and Colander suggest that quite a number of successful applicants to graduate economics departments are rejects from departments of pure mathematics, on whom, perhaps, it may never dawn that they have moved into a very different subject, with very different aims and criteria. It is not simply (as Sir Henry Phelps Brown suggested) that much of what may be inculcated in some graduate programmes in economics may need in large part to be forgotten by those undertaking real-world tasks. A number of answers from students suggest that serious misunderstandings may be widespread as to the significance for real-world processes and problems of what is being imbibed, and that beneath the extremely rigorous veneer lies considerable methodological incoherence (though it must be recognized that some of the answers on this question are admirably clear and blunt: see Klamer and Colander, 1990, pp. 26–7, 106–7, 188 *et passim*).

Three further points from this survey deserve mention, for they would, indeed, indicate serious dangers if they were shown to represent widespread or growing intellectual tendencies.

[27]

1   A student is reported as maintaining that 'policy is sort of for simpletons. If you really know your theory, the policy implications are pretty straightforward. It's not the really challenging meat-and-potato stuff for a really sharp theorist. I think that's another reason why they don't spend much time on applications' (p. 26). This might really be alarming, if such a view – which we have met, here and there among mathematical economists over the years – came to represent more than the delusions of the obviously half-baked. Let us counter immediately with a quotation from Sir John Hicks: 'theory gives one no right to pronounce on practical problems unless one has been through the labour, so often the formidable labour, of mastering the relevant facts' (1983, p. 361).

2   It is clear that very sharply and fundamentally contrasting, or contradictory, views are being inculcated in different schools (notably on monetary and macro-economics) and that students are in some cases, not being educated in the subject as a whole, or in an appreciation of serious differences regarding unsolved, or incompletely solved, problems. Indoctrination rather than education may have been on the increase, rather than on the decrease, in some quarters (see Klamer and Colander, 1990, p. 172).

3   Professor Colander, in some concluding remarks, makes the following charge:

This is the environment in a discipline in which self-interest dominates: Models are chosen on the

[28]

basis of whether they will lead to a publishable article, not on the basis of how illuminating they are. One knows as little literature as possible, because to know literature will force one to attribute ideas to others. Formal empirical tests are not done to answer questions, but instead are done to satisfy reviewers and advisers. Pay, not the fulfillment of intellectual curiosity, becomes the scientists' reward (p. 192).

This writer would have been reluctant to believe that the clash between pay and intellectual curiosity was generally quite so starkly and one-sidedly resolved by academic economists as Colander suggests. Perhaps the element of *fashion* should be given more weight. Certainly when the approved intellectual fashions, and pay, are pulling in the same direction, they will often form an irresistible combination. Anyhow, what academic economists attempt to maximize remains, doubtless, highly complex. If, however, the kind of crude maximand suggested by Colander, is, in fact, being increasingly pursued by academic economists there would be serious grounds for the profoundly pessimistic conclusions to which Colander comes regarding the prospects for change.[6]

5

Trying to Explain the Formalist–Abstractionist 'Revolution'

Any reasonably satisfactory explanation must obviously be very difficult to formulate of the highly complex intellectual–sociological processes by which, over roughly the last four decades, the blurring and shifting of the very long-held aims and claims of economists have come about. We can only try to suggest one or two directions in which possible elements of an explanation may be found. The objectives and motives of individual economists, and, *a fortiori*, of large cohorts of economists from different countries and traditions, will certainly be more or less subtly mixed and often more implicit than explicit. Shifts in objectives and motives have been from one kind of mix, in which policy relevance or policy guidance has long and traditionally dominated, towards another kind of mix in which some kind of (sometimes fuzzy and incoherent) academic criteria have come to occupy an important position, at any rate in some prominent and well-publicized academic circles.

Explanations, or partial explanations of this intellectual–sociological process may be sought in two main directions:

1 Sociological explanations, which would examine how academic institutions and career structures might have exercised 'externally' a methodological influence favouring abstract or mathematical analysis;[1]

2 Intellectual–methodological explanations, which would focus on how changes might have come about 'internally', through changes (perhaps incoherent and mistaken) in the methodological views of economists, and in how they value different kinds of academic work.

Another useful distinction is that between the (much more difficult) task of explaining how a particular methodological idea or approach came to take over a dominant position; and how, on the other hand, the dominant position of a particular approach or programme may have been maintained and protected once it had been achieved. With regard to the protection of a dominance once achieved, which represents a much easier explanatory task, obvious sociological explanations, or partial explanations, are available in terms of the control of appointments, promotions, and publications.

In examining briefly some sociological explanations it may be useful to note two other processes which were getting under way at roughly the same time, just after the Second World War. The first of these processes was that by which leadership in the subject passed from the UK to the USA. The second process was the huge expansion in the numbers of economists, and of students of economics, which got started in most leading countries in the decade after 1945, and most importantly in the USA.

Obviously the assumption of leadership by American economists shortly after the Second World War might conceivably help to explain why a shift in objectives and motives, which had begun in the USA, moved to other countries. No explanation, however, would be provided of why this shift took place in the first place in the USA, at just this juncture, that is, a shift involving much greater abstraction, away from the kind of real-world policy relevance which fitted so closely with the traditionally pragmatic inclinations of American philosophy and which American economists had largely followed until about the middle of this century.

It might well be suggested, however, that some important elements in the gradual transformation of the motives and objectives of many economists may be traceable to certain institutional characteristics of the huge higher educational system of the USA, and especially of its comparatively very large-scale, highly developed graduate schools, in particular when these were undergoing such an immense expansion after the Second World War.

It is well known how important the length of an individual's publication list may be in the more competitive career structure of the much larger-scale

American higher education system, as contrasted, for example, with the much smaller British system. The suggestion, therefore, might have some auxiliary significance, put forward by Klamer and Colander (or rather by the students they interviewed) that with a facility in handling an abstract technique one may much more easily and rapidly produce many more articles than can someone equipped simply with an institutional or historical knowledge of a specific real-world area. This fact, however (assuming that it is a fact) could only play a subordinate role in any explanation of 'the formalist revolution', being dependent on the requirements of an appointing or editorial elite. More abstract and purely technical articles may, however, not only be easier to produce in impressive numbers, they may also more effectively serve the advancement of a career than institutional or empirical studies, because they may be less likely to involve the author in political controversy – an especially significant factor, perhaps, during periods of political conflict and violence such as occurred in the 1960s. Furthermore, increasing claims and aspirations to 'professional' status obviously may have encouraged the introduction of more recondite techniques, incomprehensible except to ever more narrowly defined 'professional' specialists.

The second institutional change which got under way in most leading countries in the decade after 1945, that of an immense expansion in the numbers of students and teachers of economics, was especially important in the USA. This vast growth in

[33]

numbers fostered more intense specialization in all directions, increasing immensely the quantity of specialist literature and journals, including, of course, those specializing in more abstract analytical techniques. Such analytical specialists, consequently (who earlier, in Cambridge, UK, had been described, somewhat quaintly, as 'tool-makers') may have been more inclined to lose touch with those who should have been their customers, or 'tool-users', and so to care even less about the 'user-friendliness' of the 'tools' they produced.

No decisive weight could be placed on any such single 'external' sociological factor on its own, though a combination of such factors might have amounted to a significant contributory element in bringing about a change in aims and claims in the direction of greater abstraction. In seeking to explain, however, the change in the objectives of the subject, the most important or key factor must be the 'internal' methodological drive towards greater abstraction forthcoming from the much expanded new cohort of teachers and graduate students emerging after the Second World War, in the first instance in the USA.

A strong inclination had existed, however, before the 1940s and 1950s, towards simplified abstraction, the attempt to justify which had often begun with the crashing banality that some degree of abstraction is inevitable in all scientific endeavour and especially in analysing the complex problems with which economics has to deal – a methodological *aperçu* from which the conclusion seems often tacitly to have been drawn that almost any kind or degree of abstraction may be justifiable. Indeed, various methodological justifications have been specifically devised by 'theoretical' economists, over the decades, for virtually unlimited abstraction and simplification. One such doctrine was that recommended by Joan Robinson, early in her career, as the 'optimistic' method, according to which the economist should start from highly simplified, abstract cases, which, in spite of their extreme simplification, might serve as 'first approximations', or stepping-stones, towards second approximations, which it was 'optimistically' maintained would eventually lead towards the explanation of real-world problems. Professor Robinson originally called for 'patience' in using this 'optimistic' method, though her own supply of patience with regard to her earlier neo-classical simplifications and abstractions was rather rapidly exhausted. She transferred her optimistic faith, however, even more confidently, to the even more extreme abstractions and simplifications of Marxian economic theory.[2]

It may well be possible to work out cases where a genuine advance from a highly simplified 'first approximation' may be made to a significantly less unrealistic 'second approximation'. Very often, however, it emerges that there is no 'second approximation' available, and the bewildered student is left isolated on the stepping-stone of his 'first approximation', with no further stepping-stones in sight to take him or her towards the far-distant real world. For example, starting from the long and widely used classical and neo-classical assumption of full knowledge and the absence of uncertainty, on which so many economic models have been dependent, one can find no satisfactory 'second approximation' regarding knowledge, but simply an almost infinite variety of possible cases from which only exhaustive empirical studies can discover which are relevant in particular situations.[3] Two further examples of analytical developments to which, in the middle decades of this century, economists initially devoted long, strenuous, and enthusiastically optimistic efforts, and which both started from extreme abstractions, were 'welfare' analysis and equilibrium growth-modelling. In both cases, after decades of ingenious manipulation, efforts petered out with the level of abstraction almost as far-fetched as it had been, 'optimistically', from the start, with any significant real-world relevance as far away as ever.

The tendency with regard to abstraction towards 'anything goes' was further encouraged by the doctrine, none too clearly expounded in Professor Friedman's famous essay 'The methodology of positive economics', according to which the unrealism of 'assumptions' need, and should, not be questioned, provided the conclusions or predictions were tested. This proviso regarding the testing of predictions seems often to have been overlooked amidst the growing tendency to deny the very possibility or even desirability of testing economic 'theories'. Regarding this 'as if', wishful-thinking, permissive attitude to abstract assumptions, James

Tobin's comment may be noted, that such a methodological approach 'has done great damage . . . . My reaction is that we are not so good at testing hypotheses so that we can give up any information we have at whatever stage of the argument. The realism of assumptions does matter. Any evidence you have on that, either casual or empirical, is relevant' (see Klamer, 1984, pp. 105–6).[4]

The movement towards greater permissiveness or extremes in abstraction in economic 'model'-building, does not, however, seem to have started from any explicit repudiation of real-world policy relevance and policy guidance as a longer-term objective, or from any deliberate intention to change the aims and objectives of the subject. For some time it may have been 'optimistically' hoped that by some lengthy, Böhm-Bawerkian, 'roundabout' process (assumed generally to be more productive than more 'direct' processes) some fruitful conclusions, possessing real-world policy relevance, would eventually be reached. Indeed the exponents of more and more abstraction, though generally far from explicit or forthcoming about their intentions, at least in some cases seem to have shared an important characteristic of a number of the more enthusiastic movements, or schools of thought, in the history of the subject, from the physiocrats and some of the English classicals onwards (including, especially, of course, the Marxists). As Sir John Hicks, in his final methodological essay observed: 'I do think it is a besetting vice of economists to overplay their hands, to claim more for their subject than they should . . . . I have on occasion fallen into that vice myself' (1983, p. 364). As regards this 'besetting vice', some of the exponents of more and more extreme abstraction do not appear to have fallen short compared with earlier over-optimistic schools of thought, when they have claimed 'great practical importance' for their abstractions – much greater than could possibly be justified.[5]

When, however, decade has followed decade, with abstraction becoming more and more intensive and extensive, with very little emerging of real-world relevance, the possibility has had to be faced that not much useful or usable knowledge was attainable in that direction. Various reactions have followed. Sometimes what has been called 'a struggle of escape' has been undertaken from previous excessive claims and commitments, with a smokescreen of methodological ambiguity or incoherence being employed to cover the withdrawal. Alternatively, or simultaneously, attempts have been made, explicitly or inexplicitly, to shift, or blur, the objectives of the subject by setting up new and highly elusive intellectual objectives.[6]

6
Changing Objectives and Methodological Incoherence

Writing of his first visit to America in 1946 Sir John Hicks maintained that he arrived

> at a great moment in the history of American economics. In the thirties there was no economic work that was done in the rest of the world that had a fraction of the importance of what was done in England by Keynes (and those around him); but since 1945 it has been the Americans that have led the way (1963, p. 312).

This reminiscence of Sir John Hicks has been quoted by Professor Frank Hahn (recently President of the Royal Economic Society) in introducing a quite explicit announcement and commendation of a change in the main motives, aims, and claims of economists. After remarking that 'we live in an age of American economics' (1990, p. 539), Hahn notes the supplanting, since the Second World War, of what he describes as 'a recognizable British tradition', of which the prime component was the principle that 'the study of economics is not to be regarded as an end in itself . . . . The main motive for its study must be the improvement of the condition of mankind' (p. 539). Hahn maintains that Sir John Hicks (surely the most academically influential British economist of the second half of this century) turned away from this 'British' tradition, or this 'main motive', for the study of the subject. According to Hahn, Hicks

> no doubt was interested in the amelioration of the 'human condition' but he seems to have felt strongly that the condition must be understood. Indeed it is this departure from the tradition which appeals to many of us now. Reading Hicks always renews one's faith in the importance of economic theory as a means of understanding (and not necessarily of prediction) (pp. 539–40).

This statement may be warmly welcomed for its quite explicit recognition that a change in motive, or objectives, of a prominent group of economists, has been taking place. There are several criticisms, however, to be made of this account by Hahn. One minor objection is that Hahn's statement is highly questionable with regard to Hicks's 'departure' from a British tradition regarding the main motive for the study of economics. Admittedly, however (as Professor Mark Blaug has shown in a masterly paper) there is a considerable lack of clarity in Sir John's methodological position which makes it very difficult to pinpoint his precise views (Blaug, 1988, pp. 183ff.).[1] We must, however, press home serious objections to Hahn's statements on two other issues.

First, objection must be made to the apparent suggestion, or implication, that, before Hicks, upholders of the 'British tradition' did not feel strongly that the human condition 'must be understood'. It would be preposterous to suggest that Hicks's alleged concern with 'understanding', in any accepted sense of the term, marked a 'departure' from a prime component of the British tradition in economics and political economy, so that Petty, Hume, Smith, Mill, Marshall, and Keynes did not all 'feel strongly' that the human condition, in relevant respects, must be 'understood', as a basis, or pre-condition, for the kinds of social 'amelioration' at which they were aiming. Actually, as historians of economic thought will be aware, the search for, and even, sometimes, the attainment of, a certain measure of what can genuinely be described as an 'understanding' of economic processes, in an accepted, reasonably clear-cut sense of 'understanding', began some time before 1950. In fact, it is since about 1950 that the search for 'understanding', in a valid sense for an economist, has increasingly been abandoned in favour of some nebulous, undefined 'understanding', which is often invalid, practically unreliable, or useless.

Indeed, the second major objection to Hahn's account of the important shift in emphasis which he has detected in economists' motives and objectives, is the impenetrable ambiguity of what he describes as 'one's faith in the importance of economic theory as a means of understanding (and not necessarily prediction)'. There is, on the one hand, the all-too-common profoundly ambiguous use of the word 'theory', which, in empirical science usually means, of course, something testable empirically, but which, among economists, has come to cover analysis, taxonomy, tautologies, or theorems. (Hicks, incidentally, included tautologies and games-playing as part of economic theory; see 1983, p. 371.)[2] Presumably Hahn's abandonment of a claim to prediction is a recognition that his so-called 'theory' consists of propositions not conceivably falsifiable empirically.

There is also Hahn's elusive vagueness regarding the 'understanding' which he claims. There is, of course, a powerful tradition which originated among German philosophers and historical economists, of insisting on *Verstehen* (understanding) of a kind not possible in the natural sciences, as an essential component of explanation in economics and the human sciences.[3] What, however, has been utterly rejected by almost all the exponents (until recently mainly German and Austrian) of this idea of 'understanding' (or empathy) is the use of mathematical analysis, which seems to rule out the possibility of any alliance with Hahn.

So precisely what kind of 'understanding' is it, which (according to Hahn) 'appeals to many of us now'? And precisely what kind of 'theory' is it (tautologies, games-playing, etc.) which serves as 'a means of understanding', in Hahn's sense? Except that this 'understanding' does not necessarily in-

[42]

volve prediction, this question is left completely unanswered. Of precisely what does the theory serve 'as a means of understanding'? Of real-world processes or relationships, or of highly simplified, or over-simplified, abstract processes or relationships? Of course the understanding of simplified abstract processes may sometimes assist towards the understanding of more complex processes, but often it may not. It is obviously fallacious to assume that *any* simplification or abstraction will assist in the understanding of a more complex phenomenon. If any 'understanding' is forthcoming from many, or most, of the hyper-abstractions of mathematical 'pure theory', it is an understanding of some unreal world, which often may give rise to a non-understanding, or misunderstanding of that 'uninteresting special case' (as some mathematician has described it), the real world. There is, in fact, in political economy and economics, a very long and impressive history of simplifications having served as means towards misunderstandings, and disastrous misunderstandings, of real-world processes and problems (e.g. some of the earlier and cruder forms of both anti-classical and classical macro-economics). Indeed, the tendency of economists 'to overplay their hands' (described by Hicks as 'a besetting vice of economists') has often, perhaps almost always, followed from a failure of some fashionable, 'classical' or anti-'classical' simplification to take account of real-world complexities. As Colander and Klamer observed of contemporary graduate students (see chapter 4), they are 'well-trained in problem-solving, but it is

[43]

technical problem-solving which has more to do with formal modeling techniques than with real-world problems'. This criticism reminds one of what Sir John Hicks himself said about the hyper-abstract equilibrium growth-model:

> With every step that we have taken to define this Equilibrium model more strictly, the closer has become its resemblance to the old static or even stationary Equilibrium model; its bearing upon reality must have come to seem even more remote. It has been fertile in the generation of class-room exercises; but so far as we can yet see, they are exercises, not real problems. They are not even hypothetical real problems of the type 'what would happen if?' where the 'if' is something that could conceivably happen. They are shadows of real problems, dressed up in such a way that by pure logic we can find solutions for them (1965, p. 183).

It is interesting to find that Hahn describes this criticism by Hicks of equilibrium growth-models as exhibiting 'foolishness' (1990, p. 541). We are entitled, however, to ask what kind of 'understanding' is it that these 'models' were supposed to produce? It may indeed seem that, in the 1960s, the over-confident virtuosity of the growth-modellers may have promoted serious misunderstanding of the profundity and nature of the British growth problem. In fact, Hicks's warning, cited above, seems apposite in that, because of the very limited or questionable kind of understanding which so-called 'theory' may often supply, 'theory gives one no right to pronounce on practical problems unless one has been through the labour . . . of mastering the relevant facts' (1983, p. 361). Moreover, in claims to some unspecified form of 'understanding', produced by some unspecified form of 'theory', there is an inspissated obscurity which seems to point towards fundamental methodological incoherence. Because of the epistemological fuzziness of the foundations, tremendous rigour and precision in the super-structure may, in the last analysis, be rigorous for incoherence and precise for ambiguity.[4]

7
Disciplinary Disintegration and the Anti-'positivist' Crusade

The shifting and fudging of the aims and claims of economics have been reflected, in recent decades, in the shifting and fudging of methodological principles. It may be worth repeating that: 'The methods or criteria of a subject, or the principles for appraising its results, depend on the aims and claims with which the subject is, or should be, pursued' (Hutchison, 1981, p. 26), or as Professor Stanley Fish has put it, they depend 'on the job you want to get done' (1988, pp. 23–4). If there is no clarity regarding the aims of the subject, there can hardly be any agreed basis for the discussion of its methodology or criteria. With the erosion of the traditional overriding objective of policy relevance and policy enlightenment, the foundations and legitimacy have been eroded of most of the long-accepted methodological principles of political economy and economics developed over the last century and a half. Many, or most, of the leading

[46]

writers on the scope and method of the subject, from Senior and J. S. Mill to Lionel Robbins, were profoundly concerned with policy issues and policy relevance, and devoted some of their most important work to the analysis and discussion of economic policies. The distinctions and demarcations put forward by the pre-classical, classical and neo-classical writers (e.g. since Cantillon, the normative–positive distinction) were put forward to help in elucidating the application of economic theory, or knowledge, to policies. Similarly, when later economists recommended attempts, as far as possible, to test or 'falsify' economic theories, or policies derived from them, it was assumed, not only, of course, that the theories were conceivably testable empirically, but that policies (via the theories on which they were based) should, like medicines as far as possible, be tested before public application. This kind of interest in policy, as noted above, seems to a considerable extent to have disappeared among academic economists, and especially among those concerned with the methodology of the subject. Of course, broad agreement on the overriding objective of the subject did not produce or imply full or precise agreement on methodological principles. Such agreement did, however, provide a valuable, indeed essential, basis for fruitful discussion, which with the fading academic interest in policy, has now largely disappeared.

It is remarkable how little notice has been taken in recent decades, especially by writers on the methodology of economics, of the increasing and extreme abstraction, and the flight from real-world and policy relevance, which has gradually been taking place. Without any clear conception of the objectives of economics, and with little or no criticism or questioning in the methodological literature of the abandonment of the long-standing aim, or *raison d'être*, of the subject, a kind of ultra-permissive attitude has taken hold. For while the long-held aim of the subject in terms of policy relevance was being eroded and fudged by the practitioners of unrestricted abstraction, the ideological hurricanes of the 1960s were sweeping across the universities of the world, with especially important consequences in the USA. As Allan Bloom has described, the ideology of the 1960s had its deepest and most important origins in German philosophy, though what came to dominate American campuses was (as Bloom puts it) 'a Disneyland version', or 'nihilism with a happy ending' (1987, p. 147).[1] The strident and often violent rejection of disciplinary restraints was accompanied by impassioned pleas from the 'flower children' for reliance on their own tolerance and honesty. In due course, with lags of varying length, the thunder and lightning of the 1960s were echoed even across what may seem the rather remote field of the methodology of economics. This sequel to the 1960s vigorously reinforced the obfuscation of the original aims of the subject by the extreme mathematical abstractionists. 'Anything goes' has tended to become sometimes the explicit, more often the implicit, unacknowledged formula. Most of the advocates of extreme permissiveness, however, would reject indignantly any charge that they are supporting the idea that 'anything goes'. Such a charge, however, seems well justified when long-accepted standards and criteria are dismissed as 'positivist', or 'modernist', while no clear or coherent conventions, rules, or standards are put in their place, only the most nebulous and evasive rhetorical fudging, laced with sanctimonious preaching about 'goodness of argument'. Indeed, one finds it proclaimed (by people obviously to be regarded as exceptionally well endowed with these qualities) that 'clarity', 'honesty', and 'tolerance' are the only methodological principles which the economist needs, and that it is pompous and, above all, intolerant, to propose distinctions or guidelines which may help towards promoting a disciplined implementation of clarity, honesty, and tolerance. In fact, not only standards, but clarity also, depend on distinctions and demarcations, which do not, of course, necessarily imply any kind of veto, prohibition, or exclusion.

The ultra-permissive movement has come in a number of widely varied colours and stripes, often sharply conflicting on substantial points of theory and policy. What, however, is shared is one great enemy, or anathema (somewhat like the 'Goldsteinism' of 1984) that of anti-'positivism'. 'Positivism' is employed as a vast, fuzzily defined, or undefined, all-purpose Aunt Sally, or target of abuse, possessing the essential hold-all characteristic that, on the one hand, all sorts and kinds of writers and writings can be swept into it; while, on the other, every kind of error or evil, from capitalist exploitation to Auschwitz, can – with calculated vagueness – be attributed to its alleged supporters. Consider, for example, the very widely differing anti-'positivist' writings of Professors (1) Caldwell, (2) Hollis and Nell, (3) McCloskey, and (4) Colander.

1 For Caldwell the first objective of getting 'beyond positivism' was apparently to exhume the 'praxeology' of Mises and to defend the dogmatic 'apodictic certainties' thereof against intolerant 'positivist' criticisms. We shall not comment here on Caldwell's 'pluralist' treatment of praxeology, or with what Professor Rotwein calls Caldwell's 'flirtation' with a priorism, except to add that from ambiguous, tautological, or trivial axioms or assumptions, regarding, for example, knowledge and uncertainty, only ambiguous, tautological, or trivial conclusions, however 'certain', can be derived.

The term 'pluralism' has, of course, a beguiling aroma of broad-minded tolerance about it, like Chairman Mao's 'letting a thousand flowers bloom'. Obviously, as between say historical, institutional, or mathematical methods or approaches, 'pluralism' may be commended. 'Pluralism', however, is a recipe for obscurantism and chaos as between valid and invalid logical or mathematical deductions or conclusions, or as between statements that have passed serious empirical tests, those that have not passed such tests, and those that are not conceivably testable empirically. For those interested in policy, but are not equipped with a comprehensive, dogmatic vision of what must be desirable for society, it remains sensible, wherever possible, and however difficult (as with medical treatments and their underlying theories) to 'keep the Tested/Not Yet Tested/Untestable trichotomy clearly in mind' (see Koertge, 1979; Hutchison, 1981, p. 297). One interpretation of 'pluralism' is as a complete rejection of choosing between theories. It is, indeed, suggested below (p. 56) that academic economists should more often resort to suspending judgement when tests are inconclusive or practically impossible to make. To take up from the start, however, a position which rejects, in principle, all choices between economic theories is, as Professor Denis O'Brien suggests (1991, p. 19), 'to treat economics simply as a self-contained art form, with no relevance to the real world' – now, certainly a highly fashionable posture. 'Pluralism' in fact, expresses a kind of intellectual paralysis: paralysis about the principles and criteria of theory choice, together with incoherence about policy relevance and the aims of economics.

2   At the other extreme of the political spectrum Hollis and Nell offer 'a philosophical critique of neo-classical economics', based on the obviously damning charge that 'neo-classicism' is rooted, methodologically, in 'positivism' (which is linked by Hollis and Nell with 'empiricism'). 'Positivism', Hollis and Nell maintain, 'provides neo-Classicism not only with crucial defenses but also with methodological ammunition against such basic classical–

Marxian notions as the distinction between productive and unproductive labour (for violating the fact–value distinction) and the labour theory of value (for failure to predict)' (1975, p. 141; Hutchison, 1981, p. 295). Recent events (1989–90) have remarkably illuminated the kind of 'critical judgements' which Hollis and Nell claim to rescue and champion against the intolerant strictures of neo-classical 'positivism'. The crowning example with which Hollis and Nell illustrate the epistemological quality of these Marxist 'critical judgements' consists, as they put it, of 'a flourish borrowed from Joan Robinson', whom they quote as follows on the subject of economic planning in the Soviet Union: 'Marxism can claim credit for saving the planners from believing in academic economics. Imagine the present state of Russian industry if they had regarded their task as "the allocation of resources among alternative uses" instead of "the ripening of the productive power of social labour" by investment, exploration, and education' (quoted by Hollis and Nell, 1975, p. 264, from Robinson, 1965, p. 153). Unfortunately, boggled is all a mind can be when confronted by this brilliant endorsement by Hollis and Nell of Joan Robinson's challenging invitation to 'imagine the present state of Russian industry' (whether in 1965, 1975, or 1990) if the Russian economic planners, instead of enjoying the supreme illumination shed by the Marxian labour theory of value, with its hyper-abstract concept of 'social labour power', had been fatally confused by the emphasis on scarcity and on the demand, choices, preferences, and utilities of individual consumers, which play such a fundamental role in elementary academic economics, and in the neo-classical theory of value and allocation.[2] Certainly, neo-classical theory suffers from great deficiencies and inadequacies, but these pale into insignificance beside the proven, fundamental monstrosities of Marxian economics in practice, commended to us by Hollis and Nell for its anti-'positivist' methodological foundations. Indeed, were it not for the thought of the appalling impoverishment and oppression of millions and millions of Russians, East Europeans, and Asians, decade after decade, the spectacle would be hilariously laughable of Western Marxist philosophers and economists, only 14 years before its total, utterly ignominious disintegration, waxing enthusiastic over the prospects for the Russian economy because its Marxian directors were steering clear of the pernicious fallacies of neo-classical 'positivism', which has so intolerantly refused to validate the 'critical judgements' (or wishful thinking) of Western Marxists.[3]

3   On turning from Hollis and Nell to Professor McCloskey one encounters another of the incongruities which confront those attempting to appraise the anti-'positivist' crusade and its usage and abusage of the term 'positivism'. For Hollis and Nell the appalling errors of 'neo-classicism' stemmed from the appalling errors of 'positivism', a kind of philosophical, capitalist swindle which shaped neo-classical methodology. McCloskey, on the other hand, the leading promoter, with Professor Klamer, of the New Conversationalism, appears mainly to

accept the soundness of the methodological foundations of neo-classical economics, while denouncing,
in far more extreme and comprehensive terms, even
than Hollis and Nell, what he variously describes as
'positivist', or 'modernist', or even 'Victorian' – when
some further degree of inclusiveness seems desirable (Klamer, McCloskey and Solow, 1988, p. 17).
For McCloskey, as he has explained in a concise
and revealing paper (1989a) entitled 'Why I am no
longer a positivist', 'positivism' has become some
kind of comprehensively diabolical spirit of evil,
expressing itself ubiquitously in the widest variety
of economic, political, and social contexts and
phenomena. In 1964 'positivism' was manifesting
itself in the most sordid aspects of the Vietnam War
(1989b, p. 227); while, at the very same time, it was
expressing itself as male chauvinism (in its search
for 'quick fits to models', so 'dear to male economists' (p. 231). 'McCarthyism' was another vehicle for
'positivism', even back in the 1930s, long before
McCarthy (p. 234)). Moreover, the 'positivists' are
significantly related to Auschwitz and the Holocaust
for having devised 'the sciences of the extermina-
tion camps'; while they have long been accustomed
to 'shouting angrily' against 'open discourse'; perhaps because 'their anger defends them from a
wordless guilt' (p. 234). But why stop here? The
anti-positivist crusade must keep abreast of the
times. What about the Gulf War? Surely 'the positivists' were, once again, up to their diabolical mis-
chief? Perhaps Saddam Hussein is a 'positivist', who
is 'shouting angrily' because of his 'wordless guilt'?[4]

4   While one is in admiring agreement with most of the substantive aspects of Colander's methodological position, it is disappointing to have to object so sharply to his use of the term 'positivism'. It comes as a relief, however, right at the end of his discussion, to find that 'positivism' is replaced by 'formalism'. Meanwhile, Colander regrettably describes as 'positivist' the methodology of the formalist revolution which had emerged, primarily in the USA after 1950, which fails to recognize the historical dimension of economics and excludes relevant institutional evidence. Colander thus seems to suggest an unduly restrictive and distorted concept of 'positivism', which is also quite unhistorical, dating, as it does, from as recently as 1950. We have here, in fact, another example of the use of the term 'positivist' as a kind of dustbin into which anything considered objectionable is summarily swept (Klamer and Colander, 1990, pp. 189–91).[5]

Colander then asserts that, in contrast with what he describes as his own 'sociological' approach, the 'positivist' approach (including the approaches of Popper and Lakatos) assumes that individuals and scientists 'search for the truth, even if it is not in their self-interest' (p. 192). On the contrary, no such assumption is a necessary part of a 'positivist approach'. In fact, as Colander himself just previously quite correctly asserts: 'A sociological approach to methodology is not inconsistent with the mainstream positivist methodology. It is simply broader' (p. 191). Colander goes on to expound admirably what should, quite reasonably and correctly, be described as a, or the, 'positivist' approach, as representing the entirely defensible view that it is possible for those committed to 'seeking the closest approximation to the truth that one can achieve . . . to follow reasonable conventions that are most likely to limit subjectivity and bias', since 'there are reasonable ways of processing information upon which people can agree' (p. 191). Especially noteworthy, in view of the recent reappearance, among the New Conversationalists, of age-old fallacies, is Colander's emphasis on the *quaesitum* of *an approximation* to unbiased truth without any claim to absolute certainty or absolute freedom from bias.

Colander agrees that 'there is much to be said for the mainstream positivist methodology of science when there is an agreed-upon empirical test for the hypothesis being put forward' (p. 189). There may be a reluctance, frequently found among economists, to accept the unfortunate fact of life that reliably and lastingly tested economic knowledge is a very scarce good. There is, however, always available for an academic the choice to suspend judgement – an alternative which may be impossible for the practical decision-maker, or man of action, but which academic economists can easily, and should, resort to much more often than they do. In fact, the availability of this option of suspending judgement constitutes the main point, or advantage, of the academic position. Presumably it is feared that to suspend judgement is to betray a state of ignorance, or intellectual weakness. Some kind of less than

[56]

perfectly complete and certain knowledge is, indeed, admitted in such suspension (as it must be, and long has been, in empirical science – though not, of course, by Marxists and Misesists). But there is another most profoundly important part of knowledge (as Confucius recognized): knowing when one does not know, – a part of knowledge in which dogmatists and their pretentious 'schools' are so disastrously lacking. Of course, while in the meantime judgement is suspended, all reasonable sources and methods of testing, falsifying, or collecting evidence may be continued. As Colander very cogently insists, much of the contemporary graduate-school mainstream refuses to avail itself of some of the most important forms of evidence, by rejecting alternative methods of 'informally processing non-formal empirical evidence, of integrating institutional knowledge with their formal analysis' (p. 191). Useful economic knowledge is so hard to come by that to reject or exclude any source or method, formal or informal, of strengthening, checking, or adding to it, by empirical testing, indicates a kind of dogmatic obscurantism. In this connection, it should be insisted that, as regards economics and the social sciences, the rejection or neglect of induction by strict hypothetical deductivists (like Popper and Hayek) also tends towards obscurantism by insisting on excluding a method not used in physics, even when the material of economics requires induction if the aims and problems of the subject are to be tackled.

Colander may well be justified in asserting that

'in mainstream methodology . . . what most economists are doing is not science' (p. 193): that it is not 'positivism' either is an equally justifiable assertion if – as seems improbable – any reasonably clean usage can be rescued for this term. In fact, as already noted, at the last moment Colander, perhaps realizing that something is wrong, replaces 'positivism' and 'positivist' with 'formalism' and 'formalist' – the term introduced by Benjamin Ward in his very valuable work of 1972 to describe the revolution of form (devoid of content or substance) which got under way in America soon after the Second World War.[6]

Though Professor Arjo Klamer may accept his co-author's use of the term 'positivism', it is not clear how far he agrees with Colander's other, admirably discerning, methodological views. What, however, Klamer needs to confront is the extent to which the New Conversationalist campaign he has been leading, with its extreme anti-'positivist' and anti-methodological rhetoric, might have been precisely calculated to encourage and reinforce the very intellectual cynicism and nihilism which he now professes to find so 'saddening' (Klamer and Colander, 1990, p. 184). By seeking to undermine the traditional aim of policy relevance by indiscriminate insinuations regarding 'social engineering', and by ridiculing prediction in economics as 'impossible', or fraudulent (see section 6 in chapter 10), the New Conversationalists leave young economists aimless and adrift, without rudder or navigational aids. In such a situation it is hardly surprising if 'Everyone

[58]

for himself' becomes the order of the day, with the crudest forms of self-interest taking over. Can it seriously be expected that New Conversationalist rhetorical preaching about Boy Scout virtues, 'goodness of argument', and *Sprachethik*, will, or can, come to the rescue – especially when at least one NC leader hardly keeps up even a pretence of practising what he preaches?

8
Distinctions, Demarcations and Clarity

The purpose shared by most of the various, in some ways widely differing, branches of the anti-'positivist' crusade is, of course, that of protecting their views against criticism. The more extreme exponents of ultra-permissiveness express the apprehension that the 'positivists' are out to suppress 'open discourse' because they support the idea of treating economics as a discipline which does not 'tolerate' some forms of logical and empirical (or factual) inadequacy. It seems a somewhat paranoiac apprehension that, these days, with the vastly increased number of publications circulating, as compared with 60–70 years ago, any significant body of opinion can actually be suppressed when a samizdat newsletter, parish magazine, or series of 'discussion papers', can be produced so easily and relatively cheaply.[1] It is, of course, not mere publication, in some form of other, but prestige which is really hungered after.

[60]

(Admittedly, in this world, prestige is mostly very questionably apportioned. Serious people, however, may consider that the struggle for prestige as such is not worth much effort.)

For the purpose of warding off criticism a frequent ploy of some more extreme anti-'positivists' is that of mobilizing ever-shifting philosophical fashion. As, however, a philosopher has recently remarked of his subject: nothing dates faster than allegations of outdatedness; to which might be added that nothing has a shorter expectation of life than a philosopher', proclamation of the 'death' of some doctrine or idea of which he disapproves. Anyhow, a kind of philosophical name-dropping has recently been in evidence, with such names, ancient or modern, as 'Aristotle' or 'Feyerabend', 'Quine' or 'Rorty' dropped into the argument, with the aim, apparently, of overawing and impressing on the economist-reader that some long-standing distinction in economics is to be regarded as fatally flawed or outmoded because of some epoch-making intellectual novelty, which is now the literary–philosophical flavour of the year in all really avant-garde philosophy departments.[2] With no respect for the history and objectives of economics, valuable and vital distinctions are rejected by comprehensive academic–philosophical decree, regardless of the special characteristics and problems of economics and political economy, and of 'the job' which economists 'want to get done'.[3]

First among such fundamental clarifying distinctions is the normative–positive distinction which has played an essential role in the development of political economy and economics since Cantillon, or even since Petty (that is, since a century or more before Auguste Comte and positivism). For the large majority of economists today who are, apparently, profoundly uninterested in policy, this distinction may seem to have a much reduced role. Comprehensively denounced by New Conversationalists, the observance of a distinction between normative and positive statements has also long been rejected by Marxist ideologues eager to force down other people's throats their totalitarian package deal of analysis and ideology. The emphasis on this distinction does not, of course, entail any prohibition on any kind of statement, or necessarily support a claim to any kind of *Wertfreiheit*. For those economists, however, who are concerned with applying economic theories to policy, and with elucidating the consequences of policy decisions, the normative–positive distinction remains a useful, and even essential, clarification. One cannot indeed insist too firmly with Professor Solow that, with regard to the closely intertwined positive and moral aspects of economics, 'honesty and clarity require that in talking about economics we try our hardest to separate them'. The fact that different aspects, or different kinds of statement are often intertwined 'means it is all the more important when you make a statement, as an economist, to state clearly what kind of statement it is and what kind of validity you claim for it' (1989, p. 38). Such a reasonable degree of clarity is usually quite easily attainable if one is genuinely committed to clarity, as rhetoricians obviously may not be.

Similarly, with regard to another distinction which economists have long found of fundamental clarifying value, that between definitional statements or tautologies, and, on the other hand, empirical–historical theories or propositions. If such a distinction is, in this or that respect, inadequate with regard to some propositions in economics, then, by all means, let this be shown, *with precise and detailed examples of the usage of economists, so that economists themselves can judge regarding the adequacy or inadequacy of the distinction in question and whether it should be dropped.* Instead, it is simply announced – as, for example (by McCloskey, 1989b, p. 2) – that W. V. Quine has 'dynamited' the distinction between analytic and synthetic statements, without any attempt to show in detail the relevance of Quine's analysis (which may be negligible) regarding *particular, interesting, propositions in economics.* Distinctions between different types of statement are essential for clarity, such as, for example, the distinction often drawn by some economists, though obscured by others (including, originally, Keynesians) between definitional equations and equilibrium conditions. This is a distinction vital for clarity in economics and political economy. If such a distinction is being rejected by some philosophers as 'positivist', and as such, outmoded or somehow philosophically inadequate, then this inadequacy should be indicated not merely in vague general terms, or in terms of some philosophical special case, but relevantly in terms of particular, detailed propositions in economics.

It may well be regarded as not the business of writers on methodology to try to tell economists what the objectives of their subject ought to be. But surely methodological writers may regard it as their business, given a certain objective or range of objectives for the subject, to try to explain which distinctions may prove useful, or essential, for promoting clarity and reducing confusion. It is, above all, *clarity* which recent anti-'positivist' writings offend against, since they fail seriously in respect of clarity regarding both their own objectives and those of their subject. Most of the anti-'positivist' writers also fail seriously regarding the basic distinctions required for assessing propositions and theories and for applying theories to policy – for example, with regard to the two fundamental distinctions which we have just briefly examined. The more extreme anti-'positivists' often try to pretend that when such distinctions (essential for clarity) are being drawn or proposed, an attempt is being made to impose some kind of veto or exclusion, neither of which follows logically, or can, practically, be imposed. It may be that clarity itself is the real enemy of the anti-'positivists' because clarity would lay bare the poverty of so much rhetorical argument.

There is also another, broader kind of clarity, more of which seems urgently to be owed by academic economists to students and to foundations: that is, clarity as to what, reasonably precisely, their subject is offering, or has to offer, regarding the understanding of real-world problems and policy decisions, that is, with regard to the objectives, aims, and claims of economists.[4]

9
The Non-academic Majority and Prediction: its Primary Task

So far in this book we have been concerned mainly with academic economics and largely with one sector thereof, much the smaller, numerically: that is, the graduate sector, which was the principal target of the criticisms summarized above in chapter 4. Though the graduate sector is indeed a key sector, it does not comprise the whole even of academic economics. As regards undergraduate economics, or more elementary instruction, though it is impossible to summarize such a vast and varied picture, it does not seem that the blight of hyper-abstraction has descended to anything like the same extent. The requirements of the huge numbers taking elementary courses in economics seem to have evoked, for the most part, reasonable levels of real-world relevance. Colander points out, however, that those teaching undergraduate courses may have to jettison much of their graduate training if they are to instruct effectively at the undergraduate level, since 'graduate students receive little useful training for teaching undergraduates' (Klamer and Colander, 1980, p. 198). On the other hand, the huge and lucrative market seems to have ensured that sufficient sound elementary textbooks are available which serve the traditional objective of the subject by providing the essential groundwork for an understanding of real-world processes and policies.[1] Unfortunately, however, 'advancing' in an academic education in economics seems so often to consist of retreating more and more from the real world.

It may be desirable to emphasize at this point that academic economics is very far from comprising the whole of economics. For the huge growth in the numbers of academic economists over the last 50–60 years has been accompanied by very large expansions in the numbers of government and 'business' economists. In considering the various available statistics it immediately becomes obvious that the term 'economist' is highly flexible and ambiguous, depending on the academic qualifications (if any) regarded as requisite. Anyhow, we are concerned here only with very broad orders of magnitude. According to the estimates for the USA given by Klamer and Colander, of an estimated total in 1987 of $c.130,000$ 'economists', 52 per cent (i.e. $c.67,000$) worked in business and industry; 23 per cent (i.e. just under 30,000) worked in government, federal or otherwise; while 20 per cent (i.e. $c.26,000$) were 'academics', leaving 5 per cent (or $c.6,500$) as 'others' (1990, p. 7).[2]

Something has become known in recent years

[67]

about the work of government economists, though there is, of course, a great deal more which should be brought to light, especially perhaps regarding the relationship between the kind of education and training in economics which government economists have received and their subsequent tasks in government. The same question regarding the appropriateness of their education is presumably of importance with regard to those categorized as 'business' economists, who must be employed in a very wide range of areas, stretching right across the economy, and in a considerable variety of tasks. It might be supposed that an important function of business economists would be to advise on combating, circumventing, or otherwise coping with government regulations. In their single mention, however, of these tasks on which business economists are employed, Klamer and Colander estimate that 'for most business economists, forecasting is the primary responsibility' (1990, p. 8); while according to another recently cited estimate, 'the role most widely held by business economists is that of forecaster' (Van Dyke, 1986, p. 21, quoted by Bellinger and Bergsten, 1990, p. 702). It might be assumed that this estimate regarding the 67,000 business economists for whom forecasting is claimed to be the primary, or most widely held role, may apply to a large extent to the nearly 30,000 government economists, which would add up to a total in all of perhaps nearly 100,000 economists for whom forecasting is a very important part of their regular employment.[3]

We have introduced these questions regarding the work of business and government economists partly in order to emphasize that academic economics, much less one particular sector thereof, is not the whole of economics, but also so as to introduce the subject of prediction and forecasting in economics, questions regarding which are of key importance regarding how far the subject, or any particular branch or sector thereof, may have a useful future (or, indeed, may have had a useful past). The surely extremely incongruous phenomenon to which we wish especially to call attention is that among the academic economists, the teachers (presumably) of most of these, very roughly, 100,000 'real-world' economists in business and government in the USA, there seems to be an increasing scepticism, expressed sometimes in comprehensive denunciations (amounting to charges of fraudulence) regarding the possibility and value of what is the primary task of this vast majority of 'economists'. It may be (one cannot tell when there are no surveys covering this question) that this sometimes quite fundamental scepticism is held by only a minority of economists, and that the majority (though today largely a silent or non-commital majority) tacitly support forecasting and prediction as an essential and feasible task for economists concerned with real-world policies. Sceptical views seem, however, to be growing somewhat, and at least a curious situation seems to obtain, not conducive to maintaining any kind of intellectual confidence or credibility in the subject. For what we seem to have discerned is an increasing tendency by some academic economists to express scepticism about, or to denounce outright, what is the primary activity of many or most of their (or their predecessors') very numerous ex-pupils, who have remained 'economists', though not in the groves of academe. It is rather as though university teachers of medicine were denouncing as quackery any prognoses made by medical practitioners regarding their patients. The situation, however, is somewhat obscure, both regarding the kinds of predictions which business economists are attempting, and also as to the views of academic economists. At the same time, the issues with regard to prediction in economics involve the most fundamental questions about the nature and achievements of the subject in the past and its potential in the future. It is curious, moreover, that some academic economists insist on making an exception to their general, ubiquitous assumption of perfect rationality in the case of the hiring of perhaps a majority of all 'economists', certainly of 'real-world' economists. It might also be added, at this point, that the employment of business economists (on prediction) is surely much more constrained by competitive market forces than is that of academic economists.

10

To Predict or not to Predict?
(That is the Question)[1]

(1)   For about two and a half centuries, economists, though not taking much notice of Petty's optimistic call for quantification, shared, broadly and profoundly, his concern with policy. Until some time in the first half of this century, however, economists relied mainly on broad, 'qualitative' judgements for the essential predictive content of their policy arguments, rather than on any significant quantitative component. Obviously, this was because the necessary statistical material was largely non-existent. When British economists argued for the abolition of the Corn Laws before 1846, or for the retention of free trade in 1903, they based their arguments on largely non-quantified predictive judgements which were highly imprecise, not simply quantitatively, but with regard to the policy objectives aimed at. These predictive judgements were put forward with much confidence, because

they were based on generalizations claimed to be 'laws' and on 'theories' regarded as possessing robust empirical, predictive content. When Nassau Senior, for example, in 1853, at, or near the peak of British economic leadership, described his country's supremacy as representing 'the triumph of theory' (1878, p. 169), the 'theory' to which Senior was referring was not of a hyper-abstract or tautological nature, devoid of predictive content, for which no more than some kind of ambiguous, non-predictive 'understanding', or vacuous 'wisdom', was claimed by its exponents. For example, as Robert Lowe, a former Chancellor of the Exchequer, and a keen representative of Ricardian–classical orthodoxy, proclaimed at the centenary celebration of the publication of *The Wealth of Nations*: 'The test of science is prevision or prediction, and Adam Smith appears to me in the main to satisfy that condition' (though Smith himself expressed 'no great faith' in Petty's quantification or 'political arithmetic'). Lowe continued: 'He was able to foresee what would happen, and to build upon that foresight the conclusions of his science.' Lowe did not 'pretend to account for the fact how it should be that Political Economy may boast the prevision or prediction, which has been denied to the cognate arts or sciences' (Political Economy Club, 1876, p. 7; Hutchison, 1953, p. 2).[2] We probably would not find at all palatable most of Lowe's methodological ideas. But we emphatically agree with him that in so far as there was claimed for *The Wealth of Nations*, and for other classical writings, a direct

[72]

relevance for, and a great influence on, British policies, such relevance and influence necessarily depended on the predictive content of policy judgements regarding the effects of policies. This predictive content depended on, or was derived from, 'laws', which provided the corner-stones of the classical system of theory and policy. Still today, broad qualitative, predictive judgements, derived from what were once called 'the laws of supply and demand', may often prove serviceable to policy-makers (such as, for example, that attempts to fix by law the price of a good not in line with the 'equilibrium' price will be followed either by queues or black markets, on the one hand, or by the ac-cumulation of surplus stocks, on the other). Re-cently, however, as claims regarding the validity and precision of economic 'laws', and the pre-dictions derived from them, have been more and more reduced, nebulous alternative claims have been attempted, of a capacity to contribute to less unsuccessful policy-making without, or significantly beyond, any capacity to predict or forecast.

By the beginning of this century, however, when leading British economists, by a considerable ma-jority (of a total it should be said which could be counted on the fingers of a very few hands) pub-licly recommended the retention of a free trade policy, the classical 'laws' had been much reduced (notably by Alfred Marshall) to rather imprecise and highly conditional statements of 'tendencies'. These statements were, nevertheless, regarded as not en-tirely empty of empirical content.

[73]

(2)   Meanwhile, after the extension of the franchise in 1884 to the poorer classes, an increasing political recognition of the seriousness of the problems of economic instability and unemployment (long dismissed by many leading classicals and neo-classicals as anomalous, or of merely frictional significance) was gradually creating a powerful, electoral demand for another kind of economic prediction, which, in due course, required a massive expansion of statistical material. This kind of statistical data could not establish laws, only indicate trends and precedents, on which it has been regarded as 'unscientific' to base predictions by the more austere exponents of the deductive method (such as Popper, Robbins and Hayek, not to mention the extreme a priorist Mises). But with very few and tenuous economic laws available, such trends, precedents, and parallels provide the only foundation for much-needed, even if far from reliable or accurate, predictions.

(3)   In the course of this century the belief of economists in an empirically and predictively meaningful theory has been much attenuated. It is often far from clear just how much empirical or predictive content is still claimed for what is called 'economic theory', or whether there is any degree of consensus on this point. The changing views of Lionel Robbins, as a major representative economist of the twentieth century, provide an illustration. In his celebrated and highly influential essay of 1932 (*The Nature and Significance of Economic Science*), 'Economic Science' and 'Economic Law' (very upper

case) were claimed to possess and provide the basis for a system of what was called 'pure theory', the 'inevitability' of which was considered to lend it 'very considerable prognostic value' (1932, p.111). As regards, however, the problems of cyclical fluctuations, Robbins denounced as 'unscientific' the empirical and statistical work of Wesley Mitchell and the Harvard Economic Service, along with their attempts at quantitative forecasting based on trends and precedents. On the other hand, Robbins rejected the arguments of Oskar Morgenstern (1928) that economic prognosis was impossible, as 'superfluous austerity', which would 'suppress all hope for the future of economic science' (O'Brien, 1988, pp. 172–7). Hopes for the future were placed on the Austrian abstract–deductive theory from which it was concluded that no attempt should be made to counter, by monetary or fiscal measures, the great catastrophic deflation of 1930–2.

Nearly half a century later Robbins apparently renounced prediction in economics, or, at any rate, he renounced it as 'the sole or necessary criterion of scientific activity' (1980, pp. xvii–xviii). It seems that the fears that such a renunciation implied the suppression of 'all hope for the future of economic science' had now somehow been eased. One cannot, however, help wondering at this point what will be left of the writings of the great economists of the past two or three centuries – such as those of Smith, Malthus, J. S. Mill, Jevons, and Keynes, which Robbins expounded with such masterly eloquence – if the predictive implications and

[75]

content in their works were now to be repudiated? The operation performed on the works of William Shakespeare by Thomas Bowdler, so as to render them suitable for Victorian family reading, would fade into insignificance compared with the 'bowdler-ization' or 'abstraction' of their usually very confid-ent predictive content from the writings of the old masters so as to render them palatable to the delicate intellectual palates of the inmates of some of today's more refined graduate, or 'finishing' schools.[3]

(4) The rejection, moreover, of prediction in eco-nomics as simultaneously both 'impossible' and imbued with the nefarious intent of 'social engin-eering', will not merely cut off the subject from much of its past – not much of a loss, of course, from the point of view of today's historically illiter-ate multitudes. Abandoning prediction, prognosis, and forecasting by academic economists implies also (as noted in chapter 9) the rejection of the greater part of the work of today's non-academic, real-world economists – much greater in number, in the USA, than those remaining in the academic field. (Incid-entally, it is especially incongruous to find academic–theoretical economists denying the possibility of prediction in economics when so many of the staple classical, Marxist, and neo-classical 'models' depend on the assumption of highly accurate prediction and predictability.)

Partisan economists, of course, whether of the free market or socialistic persuasions, have long denounced as impossible or pretentious the kind of predictive capacity required by the economic models and policies supported by their political opponents. Socialist economists have long attacked the profound uncertainties and unpredictable instabilities of 'capitalism'; while free market economists confidently assume the level of prediction and predictability required for an adequate degree of self-adjustment and equilibration and reject as intellectually Utopian the kind of predictions required for effective economic intervention (see Hutchison, 1938, appendix).

(5) In the last two decades, however, not only have some much more comprehensive rejections of prediction been forthcoming, but also various rather ambiguous doubts have been expressed, or suggestions offered (as we have noted from Robbins and Hahn) that economics and economists can and should get along without engaging in the intellectually dubious activity of prediction. In 1977 it seemed that the rejection or abandonment of prediction came only from a minority of academic economists. Today, in the absence of any survey and any appreciable discussion of this fundamental issue, it is difficult to generalize about the state of opinion (Hutchison, 1977, pp. 10ff.)

Among outright rejections, we may mention first the high libertarian line taken by Professor George Shackle and some of the neo-Austrian *illuminati* (not including Hayek with his idea of 'pattern' predictions, which, he insists, are empirically meaningful and refutable). Since we have discussed this kind

[77]

of Austro-nihilism before, at greater length, I shall be very brief. Shackle and Lachmann started from the apophthegm: 'Predicted man is less than human, predicting man is more than human' (Shackle, 1972 motto of book). Let us simply assert the obvious counter-proposition that both totally unpredictable man and totally unpredicting man would alike be disastrously less than human, living lives that would certainly be very 'nasty, brutish and short'. Other Austro-nihilists of the Misesian tendency, ardently propagating, with 'apodictic certainty', the effectiveness of market processes, went on, with masterly logic, to deny the possibility, just as ardently, of the predictive capacity essential for market effectiveness and efficiency, a predictive capacity which has so long been assumed, in such extreme terms, in so many free-market, competitive 'models' (Hutchison, 1977, pp. 8ff.).

(6) Second, and more recently, a comprehensive rejection both of the possibility and morality of prediction in economics has been forthcoming from Professor McCloskey. To start with we are told in a most emphatic, rhetorical, capital-letter headline: 'PREDICTION IS NOT POSSIBLE IN ECONOMICS' (1985, p. 15). Anyone, however, who naïvely imagines that what McCloskey's rhetorical headline statement actually means is simply that prediction is not possible in economics, has pathetically underestimated the subtleties of the New Conversation. What emerges later on is that prediction in economics is quite possible, but not profitable, or 'a source of fabulous

wealth', because, in accordance with the as-if, let's-pretend, wishful-thinking methodology, some kind of Walrasian, competitive, no-profit equilibrium is being assumed, with a perfectly elastic supply of more or less homogeneous units of predictive capacity, an utterly inappropriate assumption (pp. 16, 89–90).

In a subsequent pronouncement, however, it is claimed that economists can achieve 'wisdom', a claim which would seem bogus if this 'wisdom' failed to render less inaccurate and unreliable the inevitable predictions everyone has to make about other people's actions and reactions. McCloskey allows, however, that 'broad, conditional "predictions"' are possible though 'none is a machine for achieving fame or riches' (1990, p. 133). First, however, it must be noted that almost all scientific predictions, except for those of meteorologists and astronomers, are and must be *conditional*, as are most of those on which modern technology is based. So McCloskey's scorn for conditional predictions as 'cheap' is quite misplaced (1985, p. 16). Second, McCloskey seems to be too much obsessed with 'fabulous wealth', and 'fame or riches' for individuals, or with the improbability of academic economists making quick killings on the stock market – which may seem a plausible hypothesis, but is not what prediction in economics is about. According to McCloskey, 'the predictor who could get it usefully right would be a god incarnate, or diviner' (1990, p. 126). In fact, McCloskey maintains, would-be economic predictors fail to meet market tests and are to be compared with the more dubious horse-racing tipsters. When leading economists have made money out of their economic predictions it is by selling their advice, or 'charming talk', to the gullible, not by putting their own money where their mouths (or computers) are.[4] (It seems that Professor Samuelson may be compared with 'Hot Horse Herbie of Broadway' (1990, p. 119)). Similarly the reason why so many firms employ economists must mainly be in order to give a false impression of reliability and expertise.[5]

(7)   It might be noted here that McCloskey's criticism of prediction in economics is, if it is anything, mistaken *methodological* criticism. But let that pass. At this point two misleading notions should also be cleared out of the way. First we are not in the least concerned with any questions as to whether or not the 'scientific' status of economics, or of any other subject, does or does not depend on its capacity to make predictions of any particular accuracy or reliability. We are concerned simply with the requirement for political economy and economics to produce, on the average, predictions of a certain level of accuracy, if the subject is to meet its long-traditional commitment to contribute more or less successfully to policy guidance, or to promote less unsuccessful policy-making.

We would observe that it is in the nature of the human condition constantly to be making, implicitly and informally, predictions of one kind or another; and that human beings are to some extent endowed with a power to arrive at such implicit, informal predictions without the aid of any 'scientific' effort. If the actions of human beings, economic or otherwise, remained totally unpredictable by one another, nothing resembling civilization, or the most elementary kind of economic activity, from the stage of primitive agriculture onwards, could have emerged. What people learn in learning processes is, most importantly, how to predict less inaccurately to avoid pain and disaster. To meet the traditional claim to contribute usefully to less unsuccessful policy-making, what economists need to be able to produce are predictions which, on the average, are slightly but significantly less inaccurate and un-reliable than would be forthcoming without their input of systematic, more or less disciplined economic knowledge.

Second, on the question of the accuracy or reliability of predictions, it should surely be unnecessary to insist that economics cannot, and presumably never will be able to, predict with anything approaching the accuracy and reliability of physics, or even of meteorology or medical science. It is also as obviously irrelevant and misconceived for economists to despair about, or feel diminished by such an incapacity, as it is for non-economists to complain or wax sarcastic. Such incapacity, however, certainly does not imply that economists cannot predict with, on the average, quite a useful level of accuracy, although they will have to live with being proved slightly or even seriously wrong considerably more often than meteorologists and doctors.

[81]

Professor Robert Clower once went so far as to maintain that 'if successful prediction were the sole criterion of a science, economics should have ceased to exist as a serious subject' (1964, p. 364). This could be a somewhat misleading lament unless one has in mind some reasonably clear level for Clower's criterion of 'successful' prediction in economics. As we have argued, that should not be regarded as an absolute level, or derived from comparisons of levels attainable in other subjects such as the natural sciences. The level of accuracy which could make a significant contribution to less unsuccessful policy-making, and even to civic virtue, by reducing bankruptcies and depressions, is, as already argued, simply a level which is, on the average, slightly but significantly higher in accuracy and reliability than that which could be achieved without the benefit of the relevant economic knowledge. Such a level would amply validate a claim by economists to be engaged in a serious subject; and it is obviously remote from the Utopian, fantasy levels, traditionally assumed to obtain throughout the economy by 'pure' theorists in their blackboard exercises about optimal or maximizing equilibria (which have provided such a seriously misleading basis for the discussion of real-world policy-making). Useful predictions for real-world policy-making much more often provide the basis for damage limitation or catastrophe mitigation than for optima and maxima.

This modest capacity to predict must not, however, be regarded statically. It might seem a reasonable hypothesis, for example, that during this century forces making for potential instability and unpredictability, of various kinds, and in various sectors, have been increasing, via such factors as (a) more rapid rates of technological change; (b) greater world-wide political and economic interdependence, producing such phenomena as world wars, oil-shocks, and world-wide stock-market collapses; and (c) higher levels of more haphazard, 'luxury' spending, more unpredictable than subsistence expenditure, in the more advanced economies. Such factors may have made the attainment of any particular level of predictive accuracy more difficult to achieve in this century than it was in the nineteenth century (taking into account that some nineteenth-century forces making for unpredictability have been reduced). Economic predictors, that is, may have had to walk faster up a more rapidly downward-moving escalator to stay at the same level. Factors making for increasing instability and unpredictability might be on the increase. This would mean that actual improvements in the capacity of economists to predict (due, for example, to the compilation of many more reasonably prompt and accurate statistical series) do not superficially show through, as the improvements they actually are, compared with the predictive capacity and achievements of nineteenth-century economists. Anyhow, the comparative advantage in accuracy between economists' predictions, on the average, and the 'naïve' predictions of non-economists, is not affected, and economics would retain its practical *raison d'être* as a useful and serious subject.[6]

(8) We would not venture to tackle here the highly controversial and complex historical task of assessing whether, or how far, the qualitative predictive judgements of classical and neo-classical theory contributed to validating the usefulness and seriousness of classical political economy and neo-classical economics. What we wish to consider briefly are the achievements of the kind of quantitative predictions which have been developed mainly since the great slump of the 1930s and the second World War. Our own tentative hypothesis would be that for those who accept the traditional primacy of the objective of policy guidance the reduced inaccuracy of quantitative prediction and the establishment of the vastly more numerous statistical series on which these are based, may be regarded as pre-eminently the most important developments in real-world economics in the second half of this century (worth incalculably more in terms of less unsuccessful policy-making than all the vacuous, mathematical 'pure theory' produced in the same period).

The first major field of social and economic statistics to be cultivated was that of population statistics, of which William Petty and his colleague John Graunt were pioneers. Graunt and Petty did not, of course, establish a lasting series of population estimates, which was not first produced in the UK until

1801. During the eighteenth century, in the leading countries, the most widely diverging notions were advanced as to the sizes of national populations and the direction of changes therein. Distinguished and knowledgeable authorities, such as Montesquieu, maintained that world population was in the process of a steep decline, just as Rousseau proclaimed that the population of England was falling steeply just when it was about to undergo a huge, unprecedented, and lasting increase. Neither Montesquieu nor Rousseau had, of course, any even remotely accurate statistical series indicating what the population of any particular country had been 5, 10, 25, or 50 years previously, which figures are obviously the most essential prerequisite for arriving at not too grossly inaccurate predictions of what the population is going to be, 5, 10, 25, or 50 years in the future (de Jouvenel, n.d., pp. 24, 91; Hutchison, 1977, pp. 24–5).

Apart from population statistics, it was not until well on in the nineteenth century that series of price statistics and price index-numbers (of which Jevons was a pioneer) began to be established. Other statistical series (regarding 'unemployment', for example) emerged as a by-product of administrative development. In the UK, it was not until 1941, near the middle of the Second World War, that regular national income statistics began to appear. Following the war, however, a much broader supply of many kinds of economic and financial series, in a more prompt and reliable form, began to emerge as a basis for less inaccurate predictions.

[85]

(9)   With an expanding range of such statistical
series coming on stream, extrapolation, hunch,
connoisseurship, the spotting of trends and precedents, and the application of deductive 'theories,'
can get to work, though in the absence of laws all
these will require constant checking and rechecking.
Professor Robert Clower has recently lamented:
'Three months, six months, or a year ahead – we
cannot forecast worth a damn except by extrapolation' (1989, p. 25).[7] Clower seems to suggest a
highly sceptical assessment of the contribution of
hunch, and the application of deductive 'theories',
to less inaccurate economic prediction, an assessment which we are not questioning here. What we
would maintain is that with many more reasonably
reliable and up-to-date statistical series available
even the most simple extrapolation may well be
worth significantly more than 'a damn' (to use
Clower's rather derogatory expression) as compared
with the much more inaccurate, one-off guesses
which, in this field, were all that could be attempted
before there were any statistical series to extra-
polate. The compilation of these series in the last
50–70 years has been, in this period, the main contribution of economists towards the long-traditional
objective of serving as a guide to less unsuccessful
policy-making, either in a free-market direction or
of a more 'interventionist' tendency. This fundamental statistical construction work must, of course,
often contain vital analytical contributions. Certainly,
also, considerable economic instability and serious
unforeseen disasters will continue with all the costs

and pains they bring. Perfect foresight and perfect, lasting equilibria, so beloved by abstract economists, will always remain fantasy, blackboard concepts. But it is indeed, ridiculous for academics to take the line that since it is impossible to predict as precisely in economics as it is in physics, or even as in meteorology, therefore economists should not attempt to predict at all. For if the highly imprecise predictions of economists are, nevertheless, significantly less inaccurate than those achievable without their efforts, and are just sufficient to ward off, or appreciably mitigate, such monstrous catastrophes as that of 1930–2, the economists who produce, or help to produce, these predictions will be performing work of very high value indeed. Obviously economic predictions and forecasts should be closely monitored and scrutinized. Certainly, in view of the long record of exaggerated claims much scepticism is justifiable. It is one thing, however, to criticize seriously particular careless or misconceived attempts at economic prediction and forecasting. It is quite another to deride and direct vague accusations of wholesale fraudulence at the entire enterprise.[8]

Whatever kinds of economic, political and social instability may lie ahead in the twenty-first century, may be rendered significantly more dangerous if an adequate quality and quantity of resources are not encouraged to attempt to reduce the inaccuracy of economic prediction and forecasting. For it is a reasonable hypothesis that in the second half of this turbulent century, at least in the 'more developed' parts of the world, a reduction which has been achieved, by some economists, in the inaccuracy of some important economic predictions or forecasts (below, that is, what the inaccuracy would have been, without the efforts of economists) has made the vital difference between tolerable and intolerable levels of economic, and therefore, political and social, instability and insecurity. The maintenance of this level of predictive capacity, conceivably in a more unpredictable economic and political world, may make the same vital difference in the twenty-first century; this is, the maintenance of a level of predictive capacity which economists so lamentably fell short of in 1930 to 1932.[9]

11
Postscript

Professor Colander has expressed profound pessimism about the prospects for change (in America, at any rate) in academic economics: 'There is no easy way out of the current state economics finds itself in. It is a self-reinforcing state that will require Herculean efforts to change, because change goes against the very interests of the individuals who would be required to make that change' (Klamer and Colander, 1990, p. 200).

Perhaps Colander's prognostic judgements may be too pessimistic regarding the intellectual ailments and confused objectives, of much graduate-school teaching and research in economics (ailments and confusions which mark such a significant contrast with so much of the history of the subject before 1950). Certainly, however, in that sector, there are vast, long-maintained intellectual investments to unwind, which might require a generation change. Less pessimistically, however, one might notice some signs that, at long last, criticisms may be mounting to a level which may eventually break through decades of complacency and evasion. In a symposium on the future of economics in the centenary issue of the *Economic Journal* (January 1991), a number of contributions suggest important and growing support for the kind of fundamental methodological and educational criticisms which have slowly been gathering momentum since around 1970.

Notably, Professor Milton Friedman now calls attention to 'the change in the character of economic literature' which began to emerge around the middle of this century. Friedman asserts that, as regards econometrics, the change that has come about owes much to the development of computers. (Though surely the use or misuse of computers, like the use and misuse of mathematics, can only have been an enabling or facilitating factor, not an originating factor. Computers cannot force people to abandon their critical faculties.) Anyhow, as Friedman observes, economists have been induced by 'the computer revolution to carry reliance on mathematics and econometrics beyond the point of vanishing returns . . . . More recently the easiest way to avoid perishing by not publishing is to access an existing data base, download a batch of data to your computer, and put the data through the econometric wringer' (1991, pp. 35–6). (When Friedman complains of 'vanishing returns' he is not presumably referring to possible returns in terms of mathematical aesthetics, or some nebulous form of non-predictive 'understanding', but in terms of real-world predictive content.) Similarly with regard to the extensive use of mathematics, which 'is often used to impress rather than inform', Friedman states that he has long agreed with the rules that Alfred Marshall spelled out for the use of mathematics: '(1) Use mathematics as a shorthand language rather than as an engine of inquiry. (2) Keep to them till you have done. (3) Translate into English. (4) Then illustrate by examples that are important in real life. (5) Burn the mathematics. (6) If you can't succeed in (4) burn (3)' (Pigou, 1925, p. 427). (The only objection to the wholesale implementation of these Marshall–Friedman rules is that today it might well lead to such a 'bonfire of the vanities', in some centres of the higher learning, that considerable atmospheric pollution might ensue.)

Further severe criticisms of graduate programmes for excessive abstraction and the misuse of mathematics are contributed by Professor William Baumol, who, having long 'worked with some determination' for the introduction of more mathematics into graduate curricula, is now arguing forcefully for less of the same. Baumol has observed that two deplorable consequences have followed the introduction of more and more mathematics: first, that students 'come away feeling that any piece of writing they produce will automatically be rejected as unworthy if it is not liberally sprinkled with an array of algebraic symbols'; and second, that 'a distortion of relative prices' has produced 'a spate of dissertations that qualify primarily as mathematical (or econometric) exercises whose sole *raison d'être* seems to be the opportunity they afford to their authors to display whatever facility they can muster in manipulation of the tools of abstraction' (1991, pp. 2–3).

On the research side Professor Andrew Oswald rejects any complaisant, *laissez-faire* assumption that 'research in economics is generated in a form of free market and is therefore likely to be efficient' (1991, p. 75). (It may be recalled that Adam Smith had come to a somewhat similar conclusion regarding the University of Oxford nearly 250 years earlier.) Oswald proceeds to proclaim, very robustly, the message of Klamer and Colander:

> Free markets, they say, can go wrong. Academic economics has entered into a downward spiral in which, because a post-war generation of mathematicians hold power, formal analytical ability is the criterion for advancement. Believing themselves to be an élite, the ruling class aim to create future generations in their own image. They do this by accepting for publication only certain kinds of articles, by recommending for promotion young mathematical economists, and by changing graduate courses to stress technical skills at which they excel. This moulding of the subject is possible because academic economists' behaviour is not constrained, like that of commercial companies, by outside customer pressure. Academic economics is bankrupt but will not die. University professors laugh, cynically or in self-delusion, all the way to the bank (1991, pp. 75–6).

After presenting the results of a survey of articles on micro-economics in the *Economic Journal* 1960–89, and noting the very small percentage which contains any kind of empirical data, Oswald concludes: 'Economics is in an equilibrium in which large numbers of researchers treat the subject as if it were a kind of mathematical philosophy. I find it hard to believe that this is a desirable state of affairs' (1991, p. 78).

Professor Frank Hahn's contribution on 'The next hundred years' has a special interest because, throughout a career which has chronologically more or less coincided with the rise and now, perhaps, the decline, of formalist, mathematical abstraction in economics, he has sometimes put forward considerable claims not only for the aesthetic properties of such work, but for its great practical importance. Now, rather suddenly, in 1991, Hahn has proclaimed himself 'pretty certain' that abstract mathematical analysis, or 'pure theory', faces a meagre future, which will be both less 'enjoyable' and less possible for its exponents (p. 47). Hahn describes 'pure theory' as ('roughly') 'the activity of deducing implications from a small number of fundamental axioms' (p. 47). We are not enlightened by Hahn regarding the character of these 'fundamental axioms', or as to whether Hahn follows the severely a priorist line of Mises, or, on the other hand, he regards these axioms as empirical and testable. Anyhow, as regards overwhelmingly the central, fundamental, and most important of these axioms, that of rationality, Hahn now emphasizes (as some critics have for decades) its empirical limitations and its failure to yield 'the hoped-for fruits' (long hoped-for, apparently, by over-optimistic 'pure theorists').

Certainly 'the axiom of rationality', or 'the fundamental assumption' (Joan Robinson), or 'the basic postulate', has always been the general, central pillar of 'pure theory' in economics. Any limitations, ambiguities, or fudging regarding this proposition (of which there have frequently been plenty, especially regarding knowledge, uncertainty, and expectations) have pervaded and very seriously compromised the method of 'pure theory'. More and more precise statements of the rationality axiom have often limited the generality and practical value of its 'fruits' to elementary and highly simplified 'first approximations'. Now, in 1991, Hahn finds himself confronting serious, fundamental inadequacies. It is now suddenly apparent that 'history dependence stares us in the face', which quickly makes 'analytical methods impossible'. (Of course, 'history dependence' always and everywhere has – long before 1991 – been staring us in the face, and has been perceived to do so by those with eyes to see, at least, in economics, since Adam Smith, and, it might be said since the beginning of history.) Now we are rather suddenly, according to Hahn, confronted by 'the last twitch and gasp of a dying method' which can only survive for its exponents 'by ignoring every one of the questions pressing for attention' (p. 49). Certainly, this 'dying method' has been ignoring pressing questions for decades.[1]

The first explicit statement and commendation of

the 'axiomatic' method, or method of 'pure theory', came in 1826, with Nassau Senior's Oxford lecture of that year. Senior described 'the theoretic branch of political economy' as resting on 'a very few general propositions' of which the first and always by far the most general, fundamental, and essential, was what Hahn calls the axiom of rationality, which Senior formulated in an ambiguous, common-sense version to the effect 'that every person is desirous to obtain, with as little sacrifice as possible, as much as possible of the articles of wealth' (1827, p. 30). Nothing was assumed explicitly by Senior about the knowledge and expectations of 'every person', only their *desire* was specified, but the assumption of full and certain knowledge, or of correct expectations, was necessarily implied. From this ambiguous, somewhat fudged basis, for over a century, a deductive analysis was worked out by classicals and neo-classicals, the vital limitations of which, and its dependence on the assumption of full knowledge and correct expectations, only very gradually, over roughly a century, came to be realized (see Hutchison, 1978, ch. 7; and 1938, ch. 4).

Already, however, by the turn of this century, leading neo-classicals, of most schools, were realizing that there was no fruitful way forward for 'pure theory' based on 'the axiom of rationality' (including the assumption of full knowledge) if one wished to transcend the narrow limitations of hyper-abstract statics, and to construct a 'dynamic' theory of more real-world relevance. In the middle of the nineteenth century J. S. Mill in his *Principles* (1848 and subsequent editions) had recognized that 'only through the principle of competition has political economy any pretension to the character of a science' (book II, chapter IV, section 1). Edgeworth, in 1897, made the same point. When the assumption of competition had to be sharpened into the much narrower 'perfect' competition, it began to emerge that the highly abstract assumption of full knowledge and correct expectations was required. By the turn of the century the methodological lesson was being learned by such leading neo-classicals as Marshall, Pareto, and J. B. Clark, that returns were sharply diminishing to the abstract, deductive, or 'axiomatic' method of 'pure theory', based essentially on the postulate of rationality with full knowledge. Marshall, moving on finally from his *Principles*, turned towards institutions and history; while Pareto, a pioneer of mathematical analysis in economics, sought real-world relevance in sociology and politics, as did the leading Austrian, Friedrich Wieser. J. B. Clark (1899), observing that 'the static laws of economics ought . . . to be known at an early date', predicted that historical and inductive economics would 'in the long run . . . need to absorb the most scientific labour' (1899, p. 74, quoted by Hutchison, 1938, p. 159). At least by the 1930s, and certainly long before the outbreak of the formalist revolution around 1950, sharply diminishing returns to 'pure theory', in terms of real-world policy relevance, were clearly in the offing.

Professor Hahn claims that, since 1950, much of 'beauty' has been produced by the method of abstract 'pure theory'. Since this mathematical beauty must reside in the eye of the mathematical beholder it is hardly possible for us to deny this claim. It is not clear, however, why the game of 'pure theory' suddenly has to stop now, and cannot be continued indefinitely if the only objective for economists is a nebulous, non-historical 'understanding'. Perhaps it has dawned, at last, that such an objective is not nearly adequate, and that the realism of assumptions (or axioms) does really matter in economics, (as a number of economists had perceived long ago). The important questions are concerned with the objectives of economics and political economy, and with whether a lesser role for hyper-abstract, mathematical 'pure theory' might be accompanied by a general return to the traditional objectives of the subject in terms of real-world policy relevance, including, inevitably, the achievement of less inaccurate predictions.

Two main twists or turns may be discerned in what Andrew Oswald has described as 'the downward spiral' in economics since around 1950.

1   The first downward twist was signified by the increasing rejection by some economists of both the duty and the ability to try to predict less inaccurately. Initially this rejection may have represented a healthy, sceptical reaction to previous excessive claims, especially by classicals and Marxists. But there was a failure to perceive that predictions did not need to have the near-certainty and high

precision of physics to be useful, and sometimes even invaluable, in averting catastrophes or in damage limitation. Because, quite obviously, economists could not predict with the certainty and precision of some natural scientists, a kind of methodological nihilism has gained ground which has encouraged either the abandonment of the traditional objectives of the subject, in terms of the attempt to assist in less unsuccessful policy-making; or, this retreat, alternatively, has generated quantities of unacceptable fudge about these objectives.

2 It is the second and most recently perceived twist in the downward spiral, which, if it has taken a firm hold, might most seriously undermine confidence in the subject, as academically practised. This is the growing tendency, which Colander and Oswald and, some time before them, Ward and Wiles, have claimed to observe, that is, for large numbers of academic economists to renounce the long-traditional, real-world objectives of the subject in terms of producing fruitful, policy-relevant results, because it is seen to be not in their interests to pursue such objectives. Given the present structure of the profession, advancement in the form of higher prestige and salaries is seen in some influential quarters as forthcoming from a quite different kind of work, based on quite different objectives and methodological criteria. If this second downward twist in the spiral were to continue, then, eventually, the survival of academic economics might be in jeopardy if the ultimate paymasters, the 'consumers' and taxpayers, or their representatives

in business and government, began to withdraw their support, and were to concentrate more of the study of economics in governmental and business-controlled institutions more responsive to market forces. Economic history and the history of economic thought might be continued in departments of history or of the history of ideas.

It is, however, not only in economics that teaching and research may be subject to a kind of academic *malaise*, which may pervade much of higher education in the USA, and, to some extent, other countries.[2] The phenomenon recently described by Allan Bloom as 'the closing of the American mind' may be exemplified in academic economics (according to the report by Klamer and Colander, 1990) by the draining from the minds of those undergoing graduate education in the subject, of their initial interest in real-world policy-making, while, at the same time, the historical dimension of the subject is largely eliminated, and a knowledge of economic literature, beyond some recent or current articles, is dismissed as unimportant. In economics, moreover, the *malaise* is deepened by long-standing methodological misconceptions and incoherence, and by growing obscurity and obscurantism as to the aims and claims of the subject.

It was profound, though pretty elementary, methodological misconceptions, regarding the kind of results obtainable by the more and more extreme abstraction, facilitated by mathematical methods, which led from the 1950s onwards to the educational distortions complained of by Henry Phelps Brown (1972), William Parker (1986), and by quite a number of others. The methodological misconceptions, however, cannot be adequately clarified until there has been some clarification of the main aims and claims of the subject. If the main aim of academic economics is to be the carrying on of an amusing, but essentially aimless conversation; or the propagation of some kind of mathematical aestheticism, or nebulous 'understanding'; or, alternatively, unconstrained individual self-promotion, either in financial terms or in terms of 'high status', then indeed, 'anything goes', or something like it, may serve as an adequate methodological basis or maxim. If, however, on the other hand, the main aim of the subject is regarded, as it was preponderantly from Petty to Keynes, as the provision of less unreliable guidance regarding real-world economic problems and public and private policy-making, then such an aim could be seriously jeopardized by the disregard or rejection of methodological standards, maxims, and guidelines, in the disregard, erosion, and destruction of which the more old-style, 'hard-nosed', philistine anti-methodologists, with their comforting slogan of 'Why bother with methodology?', have been reinforced by a wide variety of permissive 'pluralists', Marxists, and conversationalists. Meanwhile, however, very belatedly, it is becoming more and more widely recognized that something may have gone seriously wrong, both educationally and with regard to the nature and content of much of the so-called 'theory' now being produced. The point which must be re-emphasized is that it has been fundamental *methodological* misconceptions which constitute the main source of this kind of academic blight. Pretentious over-'optimism' with regard to abstraction, and a general attitude of 'anything goes' with regard to assumptions and the realism thereof, have led to what Professor McCloskey aptly describes as the adoption, by (mathematical) economists, of the intellectual values of the department of pure mathematics, together with the abandonment of the values of an empirical science. This kind of elementary misconception did not start with the vast expansion of the use of mathematical analysis in economics which took off after 1950. The extensive use of mathematics has, however, immensely facilitated these misconceptions, which mostly derive from a failure to distinguish between the pure manipulation of concepts, on the one hand, and the empirical nature of the assumptions and conclusions involved. Dressing up utterly trivial, uninteresting, or even vacuous assumptions and conclusions so as to give a pretence that much more is being said than is actually the case, is much facilitated by the use of mathematics: not, of course, that it is the use of mathematics, as such, that is at fault. What Sir John Hicks described as 'the besetting vice' of economists, that of 'overplaying their hands', seems to have been indulged in at least as much, and, in recent years, possibly rather more, by mathematical than by non-mathematical economists. In fact, fundamental questions and criticisms regarding the results of advanced mathematical economic analysis have been answered (as were recently, though post-humously, those of Lord Kaldor) by describing them as 'foolish', because they came from outside the rel-evant, 'high status' group, or 'discourse community'. Alternatively, fundamental, but non-mathematical, critics or questioners have been gravely warned that they must learn to 'grow bitter gracefully', while failing to understand what 'the best minds in their subject are saying' (Hahn, 1984, p. 134).

Finally, the objection might be put forward that all this querulous methodological criticism can only apply, if at all, to a comparatively quite small segment of economists, an objection which, purely quantitatively, might be plausible, though any kind of quantitative comparisons may be misleading. Certainly, in the house of economics there are, and always have been, many mansions; and there is no reason to suppose that in many or most of these mansions, for example those where government and business economists do their, in some cases, vital work, the abstractionist–mathematical blight is seriously detrimental. The high academic, or graduate-school sector occupies, however, quite a key position. Some of its spokespersons claim 'high status' for their activities, in which 'the best minds' in the subject are claimed to be engaged. It cannot be too emphatically insisted, however, that, as Professor McCloskey has cogently pointed out, the values in which these modest claims are put forward are the values simply of pure mathematics, and not those of an empirical science. Also, possibly worth bearing in mind is Professor Ronald Coase's reminiscence of how it was observed in his youth 'that what was too silly to be said could be sung. In modern economics it may be put into mathematics' (1988, p. 185).

A concluding suggestion, may, anyhow, be ventured that from any sector of the subject, 'high status' or low status, from 'the best minds' or from the worst minds, reasonably clear answers should be forthcoming regarding their intellectual aims and claims, at a level rather above the answers which have been forthcoming in terms of the altitude and quality of their own status and minds, which is all that some of the spokespersons, for, for example, general equilibrium analysis, seem to have been willing, or able, to offer. 'The best minds' may proclaim that 'methodology doesn't matter' and reject all 'outside' methodological criticism. 'Outsiders', however, though not enjoying such 'high status', may be justified in enquiring whether the 'enjoyable' pursuits of the best minds have been based on any clear, coherent and acceptable conceptions of their aims and objectives, or of 'the job they want to get done'; and whether, in fact, their aims, or job, can actually be carried out by the methods employed.

Notes

Chapter 1   From Petty to Keynes

1. It would be quite wrong to suppose that, because of
   the extremely simplified abstractions in which he indulged in his *Principles of Political Economy*, Ricardo
   did not regard the guidance and enlightenment of
   economic policy as the prime and almost immediate
   objective of his task as an economist. Soon after
   completing his *magnum opus*, and urged on by his
   mentor James Mill, Ricardo bought himself a seat in
   Parliament so that British economic policy might
   directly and immediately benefit from the new science of political economy which he was so remarkably advancing. Ricardo is, in fact, a prime specimen
   of that dangerous intellectual type, the extreme
   abstractionist–deductivist possessed by a passionate
   eagerness to apply the results of his unrealistic abstractions (or 'models') to the real world.
2. The history of economic thought may help towards,

and is essential for, a realistic grasp of the possibilities of economic knowledge, which is often, in turn, necessary for appraising critically the over-optimistic policy proposals of ideologues and politicians. A knowledge of earlier writings may also yield relevant ideas for current policy-making (as demonstrated by Todd G. Buchholz in his *New Ideas from Old Economists'*, 1990). It seems, however, recently to have become rather fashionable to deplore attempts to seek enlightenment from earlier economists with regard either to current policies or current theory and the criticism thereof. It is observed that the earlier writers were not concerned with our problems, either of policy or theory, and often did not accept our criteria. Criticisms of the misinterpretation of earlier writers from this scholarly viewpoint may indeed sometimes be relevant and salutary. But they may also go much too far if any discussion of earlier ideas in terms of today's problems is comprehensively rejected. Certainly today the vast majority of academic economists and historians are not much interested in current policy problems, in any case, but the few that are so interested are quite entitled to study earlier writers from that viewpoint and may even sometimes achieve enlightening insights. Moreover, some earlier writers, notably the physiocrats, quite clearly and dogmatically claimed universal significance for their ideas, which they ranked with the discovery of the wheel. So even though the ideas of the physiocrats may be more sympathetically interpreted in terms of the problems of French agriculture in the middle decades of the eighteenth century, one is perfectly entitled to apply the more universalist criteria to which the physiocrats themselves so confidently appealed.

[105]

Chapter 2 The Neo-classicals and Real-world Problems

1. Alfred Marshall, having been invited by Wicksell to comment on a criticism by Böhm-Bawerk regarding the theory of interest and capital, clearly indicated his priorities by complaining, somewhat testily, that such abstruse discussions would be a waste of time, since 'England is going to the bad because we English economists have not time and strength enough to deal with the *real* problems of our age' (letter of 19 December 1904; italics added; Gårdlund, 1958, pp. 342–3). On the other hand, J. N. Keynes, the methodologist of the Cambridge School, 'showed little confidence or indeed interest, in the role of economists as policy advisers except possibly in indicating "the laws, and institutions, and economic habits that are most favourable to the production and accumulation of wealth"' (Deane, n.d., pp. 20–1). Cambridge economists, however, paid very little attention to Keynes's methodological ideas, in spite of their having been mainly approved by Marshall.

   Edgeworth might be suggested as an exponent of a more abstract, academic approach to the subject. As such, his stock seems to have been rising rapidly in the last decade or two. In the recent *New Palgrave Dictionary* (1987), if one includes the article on his statistical work, Edgeworth gets more space than Marshall. Edgeworth's early utilitarian enthusiasms, however, seem to have been imbued with a belief in important real-world applicability, while many of his papers are concerned with such practical questions as taxation and monopoly. Professor Hayek (1960, p. 208) has even credited, or rather accused, Edge-

worth of having provided the most persuasive intellectual argument responsible for the introduction of
progressive taxation. As often happens, in his later
years Edgeworth seems to have become much more
sceptical about the realistic, cash value of his earlier
more abstract enthusiasms, and doubtful whether,
after all, any real live rabbit could eventually be
conjured from the utilitarian top hat. (Regarding
Edgeworth's caution in applying abstract theory to
practice, see Hutchison, 1953, pp. 107–8.)

2. A noteworthy exchange, concerned with the increase
in abstraction in economic theorizing, was that between the two Cambridge heavyweights, J. H.
Clapham and A. C. Pigou in the *Economic Journal*
(1922) on the question of 'Empty Economic Boxes'.
The quotations, in the text above, from Pigou come
from that controversy. In his inaugural lecture (1908)
Pigou explained that the kind of student he would
welcome most to economics was one who had
'walked through the slums of London and is stirred
to make some effort to help his fellow men'. By 1939,
however, Pigou had sunk into a depressed scepticism
regarding the 'hope that an advance in economic
knowledge will appreciably affect actual happen-
ings', while consoling himself with the reflection that
following 'the impulse to inquire . . . futile though it
may prove, is at least not ignoble' (Hutchison, 1953,
pp. 220–1).

A distinction introduced by Pigou at this time which
called attention to increasing specialization, including more intense and more specialized abstraction,
was that between 'tool-making' and 'tool-using' economists. Such a distinction would never have occurred
to Walras or Marshall, for example, or to any of their

great predecessors. By 1933, however, Joan Robinson was finding that 'the gap between the "tool-makers" and the "tool-users" is a distressingly wide one' (1933, p. 1). With such a wide and rapidly growing gap between 'makers' and 'users' one may wonder how far the 'tool-makers' may have been retaining any firm grasp of the real-world problems for the treatment of which they were constructing their so-called 'tools', or how far diseconomies of intellectual specialization were setting in which were to become much more serious in subsequent decades.

3. Léon Walras's conception of the relationship between 'pure theory' and applied economics was much more rationalistic than the more empirical and case-by-case methods of most British economists. But his belief that the purpose of 'pure theory' (though, in some ways, seriously misconceived) was to enlighten applied economics, was just as firm, however extremely over-optimistic:

> Pure theory is the guiding light for applied theory. When we understand thoroughly – what till now we understand so imperfectly – the mechanism of freely competitive exchange, production, and capitalization, we shall know exactly how far it is automatic and self-regulating, and how far it needs to be supplemented and controlled . . . . Then our children or grandchildren in the twentieth century will be able to refuse to be cast about, as we have been in the nineteenth century, between a smug conservatism which finds everything excellent and admirable, . . . and, on the other hand, a muddled progressivism out to turn everything upside-down' (1898 and 1936, p. 68).

As regards Vilfredo Pareto, after devoting 20 years to his great contributions to mathematical economics, he turned away from these abstractions to his great work on sociology. (Incidentally, Pareto is probably the economist to whom the much-misused term 'positivist' might least invalidly and misleadingly be applied.)

The charge of a certain academic remoteness, rather more distant than with other schools of thought, might perhaps be brought against Carl Menger and some members of the Austrian School. Certainly Böhm-Bawerk, although he served for years as Finance Minister of the Austro-Hungarian Empire, hardly allowed his experience of, and concern with, real-world problems to show through very often and vividly in his extensive writings on capital and interest. His brother-in-law, Friedrich Wieser, who was Minister of Commerce in one of the last imperial governments, went on, in his final book, *Das Gesetz der Macht* – which he regarded as the culmination of his life work – to investigate the problems of politico-economic sociology. In this field Wieser was followed brilliantly by his pupil Schumpeter; while another, later pupil, Hayek, abandoned the 'pure theory' (of capital) and moved on into political and economic philosophy and the history of ideas. Although, therefore, some of them failed to identify what was to be the most serious and consequential real-world, economic problem in the first half of this century, most of the major neo-classicals, earlier and later, certainly did not see the future of their subject in terms of the endless refinement of near-vacuous, hyper-abstract 'pure theory'.

4. In 1929 Keynes was probably justified in claiming that a considerable majority of economists in the UK supported the view that increasing public investment could help to ward off a slump (see Hutchison, 1953, p. 421). In central Europe, on the other hand, the Austrian theory of the trade cycle, advanced by Mises and Hayek, was more influential among economists, though how much influence it exerted on government policies is doubtful. Anyhow, Brüning's fatal deflationary policy of 1930–2 was related to the reparations problem. Economists, however, cannot necessarily regard themselves as free of responsibility, simply because they have exercised little or no influence. In his examination of 'Employment policy in Germany at the time of the world economic crisis', Andreas Korsch quotes Hayek's view that 'to combat depression by forced credit expansion is to try to cure the evil by the very means which brought it about' (1976, p. 21; v. Hayek, 1933, Preface). Korsch comments that 'the course of the economic crisis in Germany at that time demonstrates to what tragic results such misconceived conclusions can lead' (1976, vol. I, p. 51). Bombach, in the same work, takes a very similar view (vol. II, p. 4). Later, in 1937, Hayek admitted that 'there may be desperate situations in which it may indeed be necessary to increase employment at all costs, even if it be only for a short period – perhaps the situation in which Dr Brüning found himself in Germany in 1932 was such a situation in which desperate means would have been justified' (1939, p. 64n.). Lionel Robbins, who at this time also supported the Austrian theory and its anti-expansionist policy conclusions, subsequently recognized that his support for deflation at this juncture

was 'the greatest mistake of my professional career' (1971, p. 154). Historians of this catastrophic phase in the economic policy of Germany recognize that the deflation was 'one of the strongest agents working towards the Republic's downfall', and that it was 'absurd to equate every policy of expanding the money supply and incurring a budget deficit as inviting the horrors of another hyperinflation' (Stolper, 1967, pp. 116–19; Hardach, 1980, p. 45; see also Temin's profound analysis in his *Lessons from the Great Depression* (1989)).

5. There is a well-known tendency for 'senior citizens' to magnify the stature and achievements of the heroes of their distant youth. There may also be a tendency to see the events or crises of one's distant youth in more than life-size terms. As one who started the study of economics in the summer of 1932, when the depression in the UK was at about its deepest, and the Weimar Republic was tottering through its closing months, it seems to me now that this was probably the most fateful politico-economic crisis of the twentieth century for most of the Western world. Never has inadequate understanding and the absence of a vestige of consensus among economists been punished more catastrophically. No Utopian level of economic knowledge, or degree of consensus, was then required; no more than was to be reached, perhaps 5, 10, or 20 years later, that is, a level which could and might have been attained in the 60 years before the great slump of 1929. If the economic statistics eventually available in the UK in, say, 1950–5 – highly inadequate though these were – had been forthcoming from 1920 to 1925 onwards, economists would have been far better equipped to counter, or

[111]

mitigate, the great deflation. One of the most paralys-
ing deficiencies (in the UK at any rate) for economists
facing the rapid onset of the slump was the absence
of statistical information. On the part of some leading
neo-classicals this was an almost deliberate methodological policy. Some leading economists were still, as
Nassau Senior had said they should be, not 'avid for
facts', and markedly inclined towards a priorism.
Professor Paul Samuelson has remarked:

> It is . . . a reasonable hypothesis that Germany, with
> an unemployment rate of 25 per cent in the 1930s,
> might not have turned to Adolf Hitler's Fascism if
> the Weimar Republic had forcefully pursued counter-
> cyclical stabilization policies. Had John Maynard
> Keynes's *General Theory* appeared in 1930 and not
> in 1936, World War II might well have been averted
> (1983, p. 49).

It may seem doubtful whether the publication of the
General Theory was intellectually essential for coun-
tering the fatal deflation of 1930–2, important though
Keynes's 1936 book was for academics. Common-
sense arguments, like those voiced by Keynes and
others during the 1920s, would have sufficed, together
with a rather more prompt awareness of the appalling
severity of the deflation under way.

However seriously one may regard the debilitating
effects of what has been called 'Keynesian inflation'
(which occurred decades after his death) Keynes was
the outstanding leader, on the right side of the debate,
at the time of the most crucial politico-economic crisis
of this century. Some neo-Austrians, in the last decade
or two, have expressed bewilderment regarding the
comparative eclipse of Austrian ideas in the 1930s.

The reason is obvious, however unpalatable. Important leaders of the Austrian School had expressed totally misguided policy ideas (to some extent because of their abstract–deductive, or a priorist methodologies) at the most calamitously consequential moment of politico-economic crisis.

Chapter 4 Mounting Criticism: 1970–1990

1. See H. Grubel and L. A. Boland (1986, pp. 419–42), according to whom 'one rather clear-cut conclusion' was that 'the editors of economic journals should reduce the space devoted to mathematics'.
2. A number of the quotations in this section from Phelps Brown, Worswick, Leontief, and Frisch are repeated from Hutchison (*Knowledge and Ignorance in Economics*, 1977, ch. 4 ('The crisis of abstraction'), pp. 62ff.). These passages still seem well worthy of repetition and no serious attempt, as far as I am aware, has been made to answer them. It is of interest, also, to show the continuity between these criticisms of around 1970, with similar criticisms forthcoming 10, 15, and 20 years later.
3. For further criticisms of excessive abstraction in economics see the contributions by Morishima, Routh, Wiles, Hutchison et al. in Wiles and Routh (*Economics in Disarray*, 1984). Morishima concluded that 'the reason for present-day economics having lapsed into the wretched state of affairs we have noted above is the fact that so deep and extensive has been the mathematization of economics since 1940 that it has lost all sense of balance, becoming divorced from knowledge of economic systems and economic

history' (pp. 69–70). Wiles observed: 'It is perfectly possible for a science to be sick and ours is now . . . . Sickness, in this context, is organized error' (pp. 296–7).

See also the presidential address to the AEA by R. A. Gordon ('Rigor and relevance in a changing institutional setting', 1976) which began: 'the mainstream of economic theory sacrifices far too much relevance in its pursuit of ever-increasing rigor'.

4. Quoted from Kuttner, 1985, pp. 74ff. With an admirably scrupulous regard for the normative–positive distinction, Klamer and Colander remark in conclusion: 'We are not saying that graduate education in economics is bad or good' (1990, p. 109; see also p. 27).

5. A review of a book on international economics in *The Economist* (7 February 1987, p. 96) begins: 'At a guess, one in 20 of academic economists takes a professional interest in the big questions of economic policy. The rest devote themselves to number-crunching as an end in itself, or to arcane matters of theory.' To this writer this is a profoundly shocking statement, and would remain so if the 'guess' was multiplied even four times over, so that as many (or rather as few) as one in five of academic economists were estimated to be taking a professional interest in policy (a rather flexible concept). While in the realm of sheer guesswork, the 'guesstimate' might be ventured that in, say, 1932, when this writer first studied the subject, more than one in two or three of academic economists took a very serious interest in the great issues of policy, perhaps with more than one in two of students, whose interest, then, was not being drained and trained out of them by their

[114]

university education in the subject. My attention was called to this remarkable 'guesstimate' in *The Economist* by N. W. Balabkins (1988, p. 54).

6. The British scene, as regards academic economics, in spite of a vast growth in numbers since the Second World War, and, indeed since the 1960s, remains quantitatively minuscule compared with its counterpart in the USA. In the UK the picture is also more confusing, for graduate teaching is still, relatively, not nearly as important and extensive as in the USA. The major teaching duties in most British economics departments are still mostly concerned with first degree students. Compared with economics departments in the USA, the British system has apparently still not completely outgrown what prevailed back in the 1930s (when, incidentally, the contribution and prestige of British economists were outstanding in world-wide terms). At that time in Cambridge, the leading school, no member of staff (or 'faculty') had a higher degree in economics; and, at the beginning of the decade, there was no living Cambridge Ph.D. in economics (Cairncross, 1986, p. 23). The sole professor of the subject in Cambridge at that time, A. C. Pigou, is said to have enquired of a younger member of his college: 'They tell me you're doing a thing called a Ph.D. What do you want to do that for?'

Connected with this still marked difference in the relative importance of graduate and undergraduate studies in economics is the greater difficulty in defining an 'economist' in the UK, as compared with the USA. (The problem is apparently still more complex in France.) This difficulty of definition complicates considerably a lively discussion of the employment of economists which is now in progress

[115]

in the UK (see *Royal Economic Society Newsletters*, March, June, December 1990). If the Ph.D. is regarded as an essential qualification then the number of 'economists' in the country is immensely reduced to an extremely small number, not only of those in government and business, but in higher education also.

As regards the aims, objectives, or motives of British economists, the picture is also not as clear-cut as in the USA. A basic concern with real-world policy issues, as traditionally maintained from Petty to Keynes, is probably more widely and deeply rooted. The abstractionist tendency, however, with its optimistic but usually vain hope of eventually getting through to the real world, together with the once fashionable dismissal of any need for realism in the assumptions on which 'models' are based, have led some British economists in the direction of some leading American graduate schools. So obstinate, however, remain traditional British prejudices in favour of some real-world policy relevance that extreme abstractionists seem to feel it necessary to explain their activities with a more strenuous inventiveness than seems required in some leading American graduate schools. One way in which British economists display their concern with real-world policy issues is in organizing, and (in their hundreds) signing, letters to the press on problems of current controversy, such as the UK's entry into the European Economic Community, or the monetary policy of the Thatcher government. Mathematical formalist–abstractionists feel in no way inhibited from taking part in these demonstrations by such warnings as that of Sir John Hicks that 'theory gives one no right to pronounce on practical problems', without the considerable labour of having mastered the relevant facts.

The formalist–abstractionist blight, however, though not dominant in British graduate schools, seems to be appearing in some of the more advanced or specialist undergraduate courses. Anyhow, a recent survey by Towse and Blaug of *The Current State of the Economics Profession* (1988) reports that: 'It is the constant complaint of virtually every employer of professional economists that new recruits lack familiarity with economic data sources and have never been taught national income accounting.' Undergraduate teaching is 'too theoretical, too impractical, too unrelated to the possible uses of economics in business and government . . . some portion of the blame must fall on the way we teach economics and in any case that teaching is indifferent to the actual pattern of employment of economics graduates' (Lawson, 1990, p. 25).

Chapter 5   Trying to Explain the Formalist–Abstractionist 'Revolution'

1. On sociological explanations as to how an economic orthodoxy may achieve and maintain a dominant position, see Wiles, in Wiles and Routh (1984, pp. 293, 299ff.); also Ward (1972, pp. 28–30).
2. See Joan Robinson (1932, pp. 6–10) and Robinson and Eatwell (1973, p. 56); also Hutchison (1977, ch. 4, on 'The crisis of abstraction').
3. I have harped on this point in a number of writings (e.g. Hutchison, 1978, ch. 7, pp. 200ff.) and have been informed for my pains, by spokesmen for orthodox

[117]

abstractionism, that I was displaying my woeful ignorance of all the vast amount of marvellous work which has emerged in recent decades on the economics of uncertainty and ignorance. However that may be, this counter-criticism misses the main methodological point, emphasized by Herbert Simon, that if one is seeking to advance from the highly simplified deductive analysis of economic decisions and actions under certainty, in the classical and neo-classical manner, and to achieve more realistic theories of decisions under uncertainty, then what will be necessary will be *'a basic shift in scientific style, from an emphasis on deductive reasoning within a tight system of axioms to an emphasis on detailed empirical exploration of complex algorithms of thought. Undoubtedly the uncongeniality of the latter style to economists has slowed down the transition'* (1976, pp. 147–8, italics added; Hutchison, 1978, ch. 7, and 1938, pp. 118–20 ('A methodological conclusion')). Without 'the shift in scientific style' what may mostly be available will be countless studies of conceivable cases 'plucked out of the air', or selected for their mathematical tractability out of an indefinite range of possibilities.

4. The abstractionist fallacy has been very clearly described by Professor Eugene Rotwein:

> When one is disposed to use 'unrealistic', that is, false, assumptions in one's own abstract models (so that they are tractable to logical manipulation leading to determinate 'solutions'), it is tempting – following Friedman – to regard this practice as intrinsic to all abstraction; and it is only one step from this, since all science abstracts, to the conclusion that (somehow) false assumptions do not matter (1979, p. 1031).

[118]

5. A typical life pattern of youthful, enthusiastic 'optimism' regarding the use of abstraction, followed, three or four decades later, by mature scepticism, or pessimism, may be exemplified by the late Lord Kaldor's changing views on the subject of general equilibrium (GE) analysis (see Hutchison, 1977 pp. 74–5, 164). Kaldor (1960, 3) criticized his own youthful enthusiasm for GE analysis for having shown 'an insufficient awareness of the fact that meaningful generalizations about the real world can only be reached as a result of empirical hypotheses, and not by a priori reasoning' (a rather fundamental, if often disregarded methodological *aperçu*). Kaldor, quite reasonably opened his paper 'The irrelevance of equilibrium economics' (1972) with some general, methodological criticisms of excessive claims for GE analysis. Recently, however, Professor Roy Weintraub has maintained that valid criticism of GE analysis can only come from within the 'interpretive community' of specialist GE analysts: 'Kaldor appeared foolish in his exchange with Hahn about the significance of general equilibrium theory: Hahn knew about the theory, and knew about the community, while Kaldor instead had methodological knowledge that no theory with certain characteristics was worth considering' (1989, p. 491). Let us ask, first, if Kaldor had criticized Hahn for some simple mathematical error, say for assuming that 2+2=5, would this criticism, according to Weintraub, have constituted 'foolish', invalid criticism from 'outside' the community of GE specialists? Whatever technical errors Kaldor may, or may not, have perpetrated, he was basing his fundamental methodological criticisms, in the opening pages of his article, on the long-held aim and claim, from Petty

[119]

to Keynes of real-world policy relevance. Hahn himself then seemed to profess acceptance of this traditional aim by claiming 'great practical significance' for GE analysis, having earlier explained that a main source of interest of his in GE analysis lay in protesting against equilibrium economics being rendered 'convertible into an apologetic for existing economic arrangements' (1970, p. 1). Hahn had gone on to claim practical significance for GE analysis with regard to such policy problems as exhaustible resources, flexible exchange rates, and foreign aid (1984, p. 136). (Incidentally, this claim, if possessing any robust validity, would have required a further claim to *predictive* content, a position later, apparently, abandoned.) Anyhow, Kaldor justifiably emphasized the modesty of Debreu's claims for GE analysis. Debreu had, in fact, warned that the GE 'theory, in the strict sense, is logically entirely disconnected from its interpretations' (1959, p. viii) – (an elementary but vital methodological point which, in extraordinarily crude, literary terms, I had endeavoured to make in the appendix to my juvenile work of 1938). It obviously involved a serious misinterpretation to try to invoke pure GE analysis, which is institutionally vacuous, either on the side of a *laissez-faire* interpretation, or, as Hahn may have wished, on an interventionist interpretation. At one point I ventured to protest that

> all that Professor Hahn succeeds in getting GE 'theory' to contribute is either the rather dubious countering of extraordinarily crude arguments for one side or the other, or the *emphasizing of logically conceivable (i.e. non-contradictory) possibilities, without the suggestion of any empirical evidence that these*

possess the faintest real-world interest or significance (1977, p. 85, italics added).

It does not seem that Kaldor either 'appeared', or was, 'foolish' in his fundamental methodological criticisms of GE analysis, given his, and, it would seem, Hahn's, then acceptance of the long and widely held aims of economics. Weintraub, however, seems to favour the recognition of countless 'interpretive communities', which, as he conceives them, seem to amount to something between mutual admiration societies and aggressively exclusivist trade unions, impenetrably self-sealed against all 'outside' criticism. (Presumably, as a non-mathematician, Adam Smith would unquestionably have been excluded from such an expert, mathematical community.)

It is not at all clear what Weintraub's views are regarding the aims and claims of economics or of GE analysis; or whether, for example, he accepts Hahn's earlier claims regarding the great practical importance of GE analysis or his more recent, apparently more modest claim of 'non-predictive understanding'. Weintraub has, however, taken his notion of an 'interpretive community' from Stanley Fish, who explains: 'Members of the same community will necessarily agree because they will see (and, by seeing make) everything in relation to that community's assumed purposes and goals; and conversely, members of different communities will disagree because from their respective positions the other "simply" cannot see what is obviously and inescapably there' (Fish, 1980, p. 16, quoted by Weintraub, 1991, p. 6).

It is up to the GE community of specialist analysts,

if they are breaking with the traditional aims of the subject from Petty to Keynes, to state clearly their 'purposes and goals', or aims and claims, instead of perpetuating the chronically ambiguous and pretentious fudge, which is all that some of their spokespersons have been offering until very recently.

The importance of GE analysis, and thus of the criticism thereof, has been questioned by Professor Robert Solow on the grounds that 'the number of theorists doing axiomatic theory is quite small and the subset doing GE theory is even smaller' (1991, p. 30). This kind of quantification may be misleading. Perhaps Professor Weintraub's claim is more significant that 'GE theory is a problem of sorts for many different people. Because it seems central to the discipline of economics, or at least neoclassical economics, and because it is a high-status activity (Nobel prizes to Hicks, Arrow, Debreu, and others). . . . Much is at stake. If the theory is overvalued, then the activity wastes professional resources' (1991, p. 1).

6. Some further comment or explanation may be desirable regarding such terms as 'policy guidance', 'policy enlightenment', and 'policy relevance'. Obviously no precise line can be drawn between those theories or propositions from which 'guidance', 'enlightenment', or 'relevance' for policy may be forthcoming, and those from which they may not. Much more often than some 'theoretical' economists seem to have realized, changing historical and institutional conditions may render irrelevant or unenlightening theories which were previously relevant and enlightening (or, more often, vice versa). Admittedly there may always be a conceivable possibility that some unlikely

concatenation of institutional conditions may turn up which may lend real-world relevance to the most outlandish assumptions. Nevertheless, though a considerable grey area will always exist, it seems reasonably clear that the kind of abstractions to which, over roughly the last 20 years, such economists as Frisch, Leontief, Phelps Brown, Clower, and others have been objecting, have been, and are long likely to remain, well towards the unacceptably irrelevant end of the spectrum.

As regards what we have referred to as 'real-world relevance', though this may sometimes exist separately from 'policy relevance', it seems reasonable to assume that these will more often coincide. Obviously, the relation between 'real-world relevance' and 'policy relevance' will depend, to an important extent, on the degree of optimism, or pessimism, which economists may feel regarding the possibilities of getting policies implemented, if at all, in an undamaged condition, through the available forms of political institutions. In the course of the twentieth century, economists seem generally to have become much more sceptical, or pessimistic, politically. We noted, for example, the transformation of Pigou to an intense scepticism in his later years, from what seems now a quite naïve over-optimism regarding the possibilities of 'beneficial intervention in industry', thanks to 'modern developments in the structure and methods of governmental agencies' (see Coase, 1988, p. 21). Failures in the practical application to policy of the economic ideas of academic economists are not always entirely the 'fault' of politicians and bureaucrats. Anyhow, Professor Solow does not seem to believe that much is lost when the 'filigree' of much

[123]

contemporary economic analysis turns to 'mush' when transmitted through the political process (1989, pp. 75ff.).

In conclusion, it does not seem of great importance that the distinction between real-world relevance and policy relevance may often be difficult to draw. The distinction which it is always important to draw as clearly as possible is that between propositions or 'theories' which possess empirical content, and, on the other hand, taxonomies, tautologies, or pure terminological analysis which do not. In spite of Lord Roberthall's authoritative warning that it is 'a besetting sin' of economists to enumerate 'purely definitional relationships when they purport to be making statements about reality', this distinction is not one which anyone with a reasonable commitment to clarity should have difficulty in keeping clear. Incidentally, Lord Roberthall's 'besetting sin of economists' in failing to maintain this clear distinction is closely related with Sir John Hicks's 'besetting vice of economists' in 'overplaying their hands' regarding the real-world importance of their (so-called) 'theories'.

Chapter 6 Changing Objectives and Methodological Incoherence

1. See Blaug, 1988, pp. 183ff. Hahn's description of Hicks as having turned away from the 'English' objective of practical fruitfulness hardly accords with such statements as the following: 'I have felt little sympathy with the theory for theory's sake, which has been characteristic of one strand in American economics' (Hicks, 1979, and 1983, p. 361); also: 'What

we want, in economics, are theories which will be useful, practically useful' (1983, p. 15). Difficulties arise, as Blaug demonstrates, from Hicks's emphasis on the objective of the practical usefulness of economic theories, and his insistence elsewhere that economic 'theories' are not, or may not be, testable empirically. Much of the obscurity is traceable to a hopeless vagueness and ambiguity in the word 'theory', as used by economists. See the next note, and also Morishima (1984, p. 72n.).

2. Economists have long been rather ambiguous and obscure in their use of the term 'theory' and in attempting to describe what the 'theory' of their subject consists of. Sometimes they have invented strange terms like Marshall's 'organon' or Schumpeter's 'schema' to replace either 'economic theory' itself, or some part of it. At one time Cambridge (UK) was metaphorically prolific in attempted descriptions of 'economic theory'. One of Marshall's early attempts (1885) to explain the nature of 'economic theory' tells us that its 'true philosophic *raison d'être*' is 'that it supplies a machinery to aid us in reasoning' (Pigou, 1925, p. 158). This 'machinery', Marshall claimed, possessed 'a high and transcendent universality'; but universality could not be claimed for what the machinery produced: 'that part of economic doctrine, which alone can claim universality, has no dogmas. It is not a body of concrete truth, but an engine for the discovery of concrete truth' (p. 159). Marshall here moves away from the word 'theory' while introducing the vague term 'dogma', by which he apparently means broad or general empirical (and falsifiable) propositions for which universal validity could not be claimed. As Professor Ronald Coase has

pointed out, Marshall 'plays down what we would term "theory", a word which . . . he did not much like when applied to economics. Indeed, in one letter to Foxwell he says that in economics there is "no theory to speak of"' (1975, p. 28; Hutchison, 1981, p. 53).

Two points emerge from Marshall's early, and not very clearly articulated, methodological ideas. The first is his reserve in using the word 'theory'; and the second his far-reaching historical relativism and acceptance of the historical nature of much or most of the subject-matter of economics; or his recognition that universal, and perhaps even 'general' theories, doctrines, or 'dogmas', had a somewhat limited role. Unfortunately, Marshall's successors in Cambridge, though echoing his idea of the purely instrumental character of what Marshall referred to as 'the central scheme of economic reasoning', neglected or rejected both of the above two vital points. They insisted on persisting with the term 'theory' (though 'analysis' or 'theorems' were available); and secondly, and even more seriously, they failed to recognize the historical dimension and historical relativity, so emphasized by Marshall, thus leaving scope for dubiously pretentious 'general' theories which certainly were assumed to embody 'concrete truth'.

In the early 1920s, Keynes, in his introduction to the *Cambridge Economic Handbooks*, while apparently following Marshall's 'instrumentalist' line, described, in rather high-flown phrases, 'the Theory of Economics' as 'a method rather than a doctrine, an apparatus of the mind, a technique of thinking, which helps its possessor to draw correct conclusions'. Subsequently, however, Keynes divided his *Treatise on Money* (1930) into two volumes described as 'Pure Theory' and 'Applied Theory' without relating this division to his previous description in terms of 'a method', 'an apparatus', or 'a technique'. Six years later, in his *General Theory*, the kind of 'theory' Keynes expounded did not seem intended merely to 'help' its possessor 'to draw correct conclusions', but was itself containing or embodying concrete conclusions or doctrines. Similarly, when Pigou and Joan Robinson, at about this time, in apparently rather more down-to-earth phraseology than Keynes, described economic theory as 'a box of tools', and divided economists into 'tool-makers' and 'tool-users', they may have seemed to be following Marshall's 'instrumentalist' idea of 'theory' as 'machinery', or an 'engine' for the discovery of concrete truth. But Pigou and Joan Robinson were less cautious in their use of the term 'theory', and failed to recognize the fundamental importance of the historical dimension.

In the 1930s the term 'pure theory' figured prominently in Robbins's *Essay* and in the title of Hayek's *Pure Theory of Capital*. As regards the question as to what 'pure theory' (or, more precisely, propositions of 'pure theory') were supposed to be 'pure' of, or free from (as contrasted with propositions of 'applied theory'), the answer is empirical, falsifiable, or predictive content – though the 'pure' theorists may often not have realized the nature of their 'purity'. Thus the virtuous sounding 'purity' was purchased at the cost of empirical vacuity, but achieved in return a kind of 'certainty' which was emphatically claimed by Robbins. Obviously, therefore, it would be quite

[127]

misconceived to urge empirical testing for 'propositions of pure theory', since they deal with purely logical or mathematical relationships. In that 'propositions of pure theory' provide a network of concepts, a conceptual framework, or 'language system', with which to address economic problems, they could be likened to the metaphorical 'machinery', 'engine', or 'box of tools' of the Cambridge tradition, that is, not themselves embodying 'concrete', empirically testable truth, but helping in the discovery of such truth by providing a language in which it was possible to formulate precise questions and to analyse precise conceptual implications and interrelations. Though it is reasonably clarifying, therefore, to compare 'pure theory' in economics with an 'engine', or a 'box of tools', 'pure' theory obviously does not or should not, comprise the whole of economic theory (and I entirely agree with Jan Pen, 1985, p. 166, that 'a box of tools may not be called a theory').

Following Keynes's *Treatise* where the 'Pure Theory' of volume I was followed by the 'Applied Theory' of volume II, 'propositions of pure theory' could be contrasted with 'propositions of applied theory', the 'pure' propositions taking the form 'If . . . then . . .'; and the 'impure' or 'applied' propositions the form 'Since . . . therefore . . .' (Hutchison, 1938, pp. 23–4). In the pure form only a logical or mathematical relationship was stated; in the 'applied' form an empirical assumption was asserted as valid and a logical implication deduced from it. The application of 'pure theory', or the relationship between 'pure' and applied propositions, was lucidly described, with no specific reference to the usage or practice of economists, by Moritz Schlick:

the construction of a strict deductive science has only
the significance of a game with symbols. In such an
abstract science as number theory, for example, we
erect the edifice for the sake of the pleasure obtained from the play of concepts. But in geometry,
and even more in the empirical sciences, the motive
for putting together the network of concepts is above
all our interest in certain intuitive or real objects.
Here the interest attaches not so much to the abstract
interconnections as to the examples that run parallel
to the conceptual relations. In general, we concern
ourselves with the abstract only in order to apply it
to the intuitive (or 'real'). But . . . the moment we carry
over a conceptual relation to intuitive (or 'real')
examples, we are no longer assured of complete
rigor. When real objects are given us, how can we
know with absolute certainty that they stand in just
the relations to one another that are laid down in
the postulates through which we are able to define
the concepts? (Schlick, 1925 and 1974, pp. 37–8; see
Hutchison, 1938, pp. 33–4).

Breaking down the term 'theory' into constituent
'pure' and 'applied' propositions might have some
clarifying potential, though it would show up how
much 'pure' theory was being created which seldom
if ever got 'applied', quite often because it was simply
inapplicable. Meanwhile, however, the influence of
Popper and Lakatos, whose original and main interests
were in the more highly developed natural sciences,
encouraged excessive emphasis on a conception of
theory derived from a hypothetico–deductive method,
highly successful in physics, of course, but not suited
to much of the material of economics with its vital,
non-static, historical dimension. The hypothetical–
deductive method had, up to a point, seemed to have

proved itself fruitful in the development of neo-classical economics, but its basic postulates, in particular those concerned with knowledge, never had the solid validity of their natural-scientific counterparts. Such exponents of a priorism as Mises and Knight (together with Robbins and Hayek in their earlier days in the early and mid 1930s) claimed, however, that the basic postulates of economic theory, based on introspection, were more solid and unquestionable than those of the natural sciences, thus again overlooking the vital historical dimension of any economics which sought to get beyond the abstractions of statics.

Later, mainly after 1945, ambiguity and illusion were further heightened by the introduction of the term 'model', a masterpiece of intellectual conjuring which has veiled the most hyper-abstract, unrealistic over-simplifications with a pretence of some resemblance or relevance to reality.

Turning to Hicks, we find him harking back to the Cambridge notion of economic theory as 'machinery', a 'box of tools', or, as Keynes put it, an 'apparatus of the mind' (a phrase quoted by Hicks; see Blaug, 1988, p. 185). Since, as the Cambridge authorities repeatedly emphasized, economic 'theory', in their sense, does not contain 'concrete truth', but is purely auxiliary to its discovery, it was, of course, quite consequential of Hicks to reject any testing or falsifiability of 'economic theory', or rather of 'pure theory'. It is also clear why Hicks can describe 'much' of economic theory as a game, and include tautologies as a part of 'theory'. Though it might be hoped, however, and may seem implied, that there is another component of 'economic theory', which is not simply either auxiliary, tautological, a game, or empirically vacuous, it is not clear from Hicks just what this component consists of. He makes no use of the concept of 'applied theory', which is where falsifiable formulations and empirical testing would be relevant.

Certainly in his later writings Hicks does insist on the historical dimension of any economic theory getting beyond static abstractions. Surely, however, the necessity for more and more tests, or more constantly repeated tests, has to be recognized, the more mere statics are transcended by attempts to cope with historical–institutional change. Hicks's other objective of 'practically useful' theories, which should be 'the servant of applied economics', points to the same requirement of testing and testability (Blaug, 1988, p. 188; Hicks, 1983, pp. 15, 361). It remains difficult, however, to resist Mark Blaug's conclusion regarding the impossibility of extracting 'any coherent methodology from the writings of Hicks' (1988, p. 194).

3. Quite unnecessarily extreme conclusions have been drawn with regard to the profundity of the differences between the social and human disciplines and the natural sciences by those emphasizing the interest or importance of 'understanding', or *Verstehen*.

4. Regarding the fundamental 'axioms' of general equilibrium analysis, Professor Hahn has assured us that 'good theorists devote much care and attention to the formulation of these axioms' (1984, p. 7). Well good theorists would, wouldn't they? (whatever it is, precisely, that 'good theorists' are engaged in). Again Hahn assures us that 'serious theory . . . provides quite clearly the documentation of its own inadequacies and incompleteness' (p. 333). Again, 'serious theory'

[131]

would, wouldn't it? (whatever 'serious theory' precisely consists of – games-playing, tautologies, pure terminological analysis, or whatever else). Nevertheless, in his discerning paper, 'Frank Hahn's struggle of escape', Professor Brian Loasby describes as 'frankly incredible' Hahn's claim regarding general equilibrium analysis that 'the axioms have summed up what one regards as pretty secure empirical knowledge' (1989, pp. 119ff.). It seems that Hahn's 'struggle of escape' or 'progressive disenchantment' (as Loasby describes it) from (or with) earlier, excessive claims for general equilibrium analysis, may still have some way to go. Rapid changes of view may, however, be under way (see 'Postscript', pp. 93–7). Incidentally, Hahn may be following Kaldor's rejection of an immature enthusiasm for the abstractions of GE analysis by reverting to earlier scepticism on his own part which inspired him to remark, when referring to some equilibrium models: 'It cannot be denied that there is something scandalous in the spectacle of so many people refining the analyses of economic states which they give no reason to suppose will ever, or have ever, come about. It is also probably dangerous' (1970, p. 1).

Chapter 7 Disciplinary Disintegration and the Anti-'positivist' Crusade

1. I am indebted to Denis O'Brien for referring me to Allan Bloom's work.
2. Another comprehensive and fundamental attack on neo-classical economics has been launched by Professor Philip Mirowski in his books *Against Mechanism* (1988) and *More Heat than Light* (1989).

Mirowski's rhetorical tactics are characterized by the presentation of a tremendous array of learning and references on the subjects of mechanics and physics, overawed by which lamentably over-specialized economists may be rendered ready for surrender to the wholesale condemnation of neo-classical economists. Mirowski, however, nowhere demonstrates how the references, by a few neo-classical economists, to physics and mechanics actually come through to vitiate significantly any particular neo-classical propositions regarding economic theory or policy. Admittedly, it might reasonably be argued that an excessively facile resort, by some neo-classical writers, to self-adjusting and self-equilibrating processes, made for excessive over-simplifications, in some cases, with regard to neo-classical theories and policies. This weakness, however, is completely accounted for by the often implicit over-simplifications brought about by the essential, all-pervading basic postulate (or 'axiom') regarding full knowledge, correct expectations, and the absence of uncertainty, compared with which the effects of mechanical and physical references were extremely superficial. It was certainly not any metaphors or references to mechanical and physical processes, by the neo-classicals, which led to the all-pervasive assumption or axiom excluding ignorance and uncertainty. As F. H. Knight long ago indicated, it was the fundamental assumption excluding ignorance and uncertainty – explicitly introduced by Ricardo – which turned decision-making in classical and neo-classical models into automatic or mechanical processes. (For comprehensive criticism of Mirowski's views see the trenchant appraisals of Kevin Hoover, Varian, Walker, and Coats (all 1991).)

[133]

It is interesting that closely similar rhetorical tactics have been employed by Professor D. McCloskey, Mirowski's fellow New Conversationalist, who put on a tremendous parade of literary – critical – philosophical learning as a kind of rhetorical softening-up process for excessively specialized economists, who are then, apparently, expected to capitulate before McCloskey's all-embracing condemnations of 'positivism', with which are associated, 'modernism', male chauvinism, McCarthyism and Hitlerism. In fact, as Stanley Fish pointed out, nothing follows for the methodology of economics from all the vast claims by the New Conversationalists regarding the all-pervasiveness of 'rhetoric'.

Certainly there may be some economists who find the study of 'rhetoric' in economics *quite* interesting, though not many are likely to find it *very* interesting, if they regard the prime objective of their subject as the discovery of not-too-unreliable, real-world, policy-relevant conclusions. For the empirical reliability or unreliability of such conclusions is not affected, one way or the other, by the rhetoric (in any normal sense of the term) by which they may be accompanied. Admittedly, however, this proviso with regard to economists' views on the prime aim or objective of their subject may not now hold good over wide areas of academic, or graduate-school economics (see the following note 3 and note 3 of ch. 8). On the fudging by New Conversationalists of the distinction between persuasion and justification, see Rosenberg (1988a).

3. Whether the total collapse of the Marxian economies in Eastern Europe and the Soviet Union will be followed by serious, major revisions or even partial

retractions on the part of academic Marxist economists in the West remains doubtful. Certainly no impression of any fundamental rethinking is to be detected in the very numerous and extensive Marxist and Marxo-Sraffian contributions to the *New Palgrave Dictionary* (1987) for which a high degree of up-to-dateness was claimed when it appeared right on the brink of the economic collapses in the East. The utter failure in the real world of the Marxist economies is presumably regarded as totally irrelevant by Marxo-Sraffian theorists, who would firmly reject the admissibility of questions now being asked, not merely about Marx after Sraffa, but about *Marx and Sraffa after 1989–90.* A few decades back, Western academic Marxists, like Maurice Dobb, Joan Robinson, Ronald Meek, and the (marginally Marxist) Lord Balogh, were inspired and driven by their high, Utopian claims and hopes regarding the progress of the Marxist–Communist economy of the Soviet Union, which they represented as, in crucial respects, an essentially Marxist model, or example, for Western and other economies around the world, with regard, for example, to food and agricultural production, and to the planning of investment. A leading Marxist academic economist in the UK, for example, claimed (in 1954) that the Soviet Union's great plans for the increase of food production 'are making a mockery of the Malthusian theory of population and the law of diminishing returns'. As late as 1963 a socialist economic expert (who in the following year became Economic Adviser to the British Prime Minister) in recommending that centralized investment controls should be imposed in order to raise the British rate of growth to 5–5½ per cent, observed: 'This was the way the

[135]

Soviet obtained its results, and I doubt whether we can do better.'

About the same time, one of the leading Marxist authorities in Cambridge (UK), though conceding that Western capitalism might manage to stagger on (in spite of Marxist predictions of its incipient collapse) proclaimed that the Western system of capitalism could only survive as 'the second best economic system in the world', that is, as far inferior to the system of the Soviet Union, China, North Korea, etc. Blackly farcical though such claims and pronouncements may seem today, those who uttered them were at least undeniably concerned, after their fashion, with real-world processes and policies, as they envisaged them, not with pure abstractions. In the last decade or two, however, as real-world hopes and claims for the Eastern economies have become increasingly impossible to sustain, even by Western, *Marxisant* academics, an increasing retreat has been undertaken into the kind of other-worldly hyper-abstractions so fashionable among bourgeois academics. Marxo-Sraffianism has provided a rarefied, esoteric safe haven for those Marxist economists who find it impossible to confront any longer the realities of the Marxist economies around much of the world. Moreover, hyper-abstract Marxist 'model-building', when generously sprinkled with mathematical symbols, may appear to take on much of the same kind of intellectual respectability as that exuded by ortho-dox or 'mainstream' academic sources.

Doubtless the Marxian version of the history of economic thought will still be energetically promoted, with the supposedly proto-Marxist 'production-oriented approach' extolled, together with the labour and cost-of-production theory of value, as contrasted with the pre-classical and neo-classical subjective value theory, based on the concepts of individual utility, choice, and demand – so tainted, according to Marxists, by what the prophet described as 'bad conscience and the evil intent of apologetic'. The fact that it was precisely 'the production-oriented approach', with its rejection of individual utility, choice, and demand, which brought about, fundamentally, in the long run, the collapse of the Marxist economies, may be shrugged off by Western Marxists, just as the monstrosities of Stalin were still being shrugged off by Western Marxists down to and even long after his death. Nor can any optimism be entertained that the fundamental irresponsibility, which has come down directly from Marx himself, will be abandoned, of demanding, and campaigning for, the violent and total overthrow of the existing system by Marxists who possess no serious ideas regarding an alternative system even remotely less unsatisfactory.

4. Anyone attempting to appraise the ideas of McCloskey and the New Conversationalists is confronted by the stark contrasts and inconsistencies between various versions of their views.

(a) Let us take, first, McCloskey's view, or concept, of 'positivism'. In the second edition of McCloskey's explanation 'Why I am no longer a positivist' (1989b), all the above-quoted suggestions are retained regarding 'positivism' and the Vietnam War, McCarthyism, male chauvinism, and Auschwitz. Apparently, however, to guard against charges of slight exaggeration, the not very convincing disclaimer is inserted: 'I am not claiming that positivists are fascists' (p. 234).

McCloskey even conceded, with remarkable gener-
osity: 'I do not regard positivism as a useless or silly
movement. In its time it did a great deal of good'
(p. 226). In conclusion, nevertheless, McCloskey
maintains: 'Positivism is not, in short, a philosophy
for an adult in science. Young men – especially *men*
– can believe it because they can believe any crazy
thing.' McCloskey explains, in fact, that he is no longer
a 'positivist', by reminding us that he is now grown
up because he 'was able to put away his childish
toys' (p. 237). Certainly if McCloskey's treatment of
'positivism' is not an example of 'anything goes', it is
impossible to say what would be.

(b)   A second bewildering contrast appears between
the lofty moral claims of the New Conversationalists,
and the actual performances. The concluding perora-
tion of *The Rhetoric of Economics* (1985) proclaimed
that 'rhetoric', or the New Conversation, would 'improve the temper of economists' by rising above 'the
bitterness beyond reason', with which 'an overblown
methodology' had served to 'spoil the conversation'
(1985, pp. 183–4). In a subsequent, morally uplifting
joint statement, McCloskey and Klamer claimed some
significant resemblance between the standards of the
New Conversationalists and the ideals of Boy Scouts:
'Being a good conversationalist asks far more than
does following some method. Alarmingly it asks for
goodness . . . goodness in the usual scout handbook
sense: honesty, bravery, tolerance, consideration . . . .
A rhetoric of economics . . . encourages admirable
goodness in argument all round' (Klamer, McCloskey,
and Solow, 1988, pp. 16, 18). Presumably, in trying
to associate 'positivists' (or those who criticize him,

or with whom he disagrees) with the Vietnam War, McCarthyism, male chauvinism, and Auschwitz, etc., Professor McCloskey was demonstrating his commitment to 'tolerance', 'consideration', and '*Sprachethik*', and to encouraging 'goodness in argument' all round. McCloskey, with amusing modesty, seems to like casting himself in the role of Socrates. Those, however, who find themselves confronted with his New Conversationalist rhetoric seem to perceive rather the conversational style of Alice's Red Queen ('shouting angrily'). See John Komlos and Richard Landes (1991, 'Alice to the Red Queen: imperious econometrics' – a rejoinder to McCloskey, 1991a).

(c) Thirdly, the remarkable contrasts and contradictions in the New Conversationalist rhetoric do not only relate to its tone but to fundamental issues of substance. Right from the beginning of the main, original ur-text of the New Conversationalism (McCloskey, 1985), incoherence is more or less systemic, built into the rhetorical tactics. First the obviously nebulous, shifting Aunt Sally of 'modernism' is set up and then the 'modernist' stance on some vital issue – falsification or prediction – is comprehensively denounced root and branch, as though some great new challenge has been issued. Anything from one to 40 pages later, however, a somersault is performed: that is, falsification, written off as 'not cogent' and itself 'falsified' (1985, pp. 13–15), is subsequently (p. 56) declared to provide 'a powerful test' and recommended for application – though not, of course, completely unproblematic. Similarly (p. 15) prediction is stated to be 'not possible in economics', only for it to be claimed subsequently that economic

[139]

prediction earns normal returns (which might, of course, be quite high) (see 1985, pp. 16 and 90; and on McCloskey's views on prediction, see below pp. 160–2).

Ambivalence and contradiction are more broadly demonstrated by comparing the strident denunciations of the influence of 'modernism' and 'positivism' in the opening chapter, 'The poverty of modernism', and the complacency regarding the state of the subject displayed in the closing chapter. On p. 4 the dire warning is issued that thanks to the all-too-influential 'positivists', economists are 'prone now to fanaticism and intolerance'. Later we are assured: 'Economics at present is, in fact, moderately well off . . . . It seems to know in any case approximately where to step' (p. 170). Why then all the shouting about the vital importance of recognizing 'rhetoric', if there was nothing fundamentally or seriously wrong?

Incoherence in the New Conversation became increasingly apparent when something like a major retreat got under way at the conference on 'The Consequences of Economic Rhetoric' (1986), attended by leading economists, including a Nobel laureate, several of whose papers were not included in the report of the conference (Klamer, McCloskey, and Solow, 1988). 'Positivism is dead, we all agree' was a recurring theme of this conference, announced by Cristina Bicchieri (1988, p. 100). What precisely these words are meant to mean remains, of course, obscure. According, however, to Professor Klamer's closing address to the conference, with the death of positivism 'certainty' was gone: 'There are no definite episte-mological standards, such as consistency and corre-spondence with facts, by which we can establish the truth and henceforth the objectivity or positivity, of a particular proposition' (Klamer, McCloskey, and Solow, 1988, p. 267). (One would like to know who the 'we' were – apart from New Conversationalists, Marxists, and a priorists like Mises – who last claimed 'certainty' for the propositions of an empirical and partly historical science? Popper, for example, recently held to be the most influential philosopher among economists, has long insisted that science is based on 'conjectures' and attempts to refute them: 'The empirical basis of objective science does not rest upon solid bedrock. The bold structure of its theories rises, as it were, above a swamp. The piles are driven down from above into the swamp, but not down to any natural or "given" base' (1959, p. 111; quoted by Backhouse, 1991b, p. 14).)

Anyhow, it began to emerge at the conference that the proclaimed 'death' of 'positivism, like the prematurely reported death of Mark Twain, was something of an exaggeration. A disappointed Klamer discovered that although some academic philosophers thought that they had cut off 'positivism's' life-support system, it was alive and kicking among economists: 'The philosophical death of positivism notwithstanding, economists often seem to argue as if positivism were still alive . . . . Without hesitation, they keep drawing the same old distinctions, relegating the final authority to the "facts" and "logic"' (p. 267). A macabre condition of economic life after philosophical death had revealed itself; or, as in the words of the old song: 'He's dead but he won't lie down.' As the significance of this phenomenon began to sink in, Klamer felt constrained to announce, in his concluding paragraphs, what seemed to amount to a possibly

[141]

far-reaching retreat: 'I have come to recognize that those of us who are eager to advance the new conversation may overlook the contribution of the conventional methodology. The investigation of the logic of economic theories is important and we may not need to deny the realism of scientific objects' (p. 277). One cannot refrain from Thomas Carlyle's answer 'By Gad, she'd better', when Margaret Fuller had graciously conceded: 'I accept the Universe.'

That the New Conversationalism had begun to come round to accepting the universe (at least intermittently) became apparent in McCloskey's next book (1990), at the beginning of which he announced the setting up of a 'rhetorical tetrad: fact, logic, metaphor and story' (p. 1). At least 'fact' and 'logic' seemed now to be given a definite status previously left highly questionable. The fundamental crucial question had now to be faced, however, as to which of the two pairs of criteria in the 'tetrad' were to have final authority in the cases of conflict which obviously arise. This decisive question is for much of the time evaded. The four components of the 'tetrad' are set out in alphabetical order, and it seems to be implied, at first at any rate, that they have the same authority, which they exercise reciprocally: 'Each part of the tetrad . . . places limits on the excesses of the others' (p. 4). It is easy to see how facts may (and should) check the excesses of a good story. For example, in a recent review of Ronald Reagan's autobiography the ex-President is referred to, rightly or wrongly, as 'giving more attention to a good story than to facts' (*New York Times Book Review*, 18 November 1990). (It should, perhaps, be mentioned that Mr Reagan has, of course, never claimed to have been professionally engaged in any kind of empirical or historical discipline.)

McCloskey goes on, rather otiosely, to inform us that 'the story of the Aryan race . . . needed criticism' (1990, p. 4). But he fails to specify the kind of criticism which this story needed, or which part of his 'tetrad' should have been brought to bear. The grounds, of course, on which this 'story' first needed criticism were those of its crimes *against facts* (criticism, incidentally, which was admirably provided in the 1930s by the English authorities, Huxley, Haddon, and Carr-Saunders (1936), whose maxim 'the essence of science is the appeal to fact' was quoted in my book of 1938, p. 11).

Meanwhile, as Klamer was so disappointed to have to recognize, many economists when having to decide between a good story and well-tested facts, have generally supported the principle of 'relegating final authority to "the facts"', while, at the same time rejecting the reverse process of relegating final authority to a good story and allowing it to 'kill' well-tested facts. It is a delightful surprise to find McCloskey, after his initial evasions, 80 pages later firmly insisting on this moribund 'positivist' principle so deplored by Klamer. McCloskey makes it clear that 'the goodness or badness of stories' can and should be tested [*sic*] against facts [*sic*: no quotes]: 'Facts of course constrain a story', McCloskey insists (1990, p. 83): 'The empiricist tradition since Bacon has put great emphasis on facts testing story. No one could object' – except, of course, Klamer and McCloskey himself five years previously (see 1985, pp. 29–5, 48–9). Now McCloskey maintains: 'The facts are there' (without

[143]

quotation marks) 'killing the story or giving it life' (1990, p. 83).

The idea of facts 'being there', and 'checking', 'testing', 'killing', or 'giving life' to stories is, of course, outright positivism and all the better for it. A vital demarcation or trichotomy is implied between stories 'killed' by facts; given life by facts; or not yet given life or death. McCloskey even seems to be going over the top, and indulging in what Lakatos called 'naïve falsificationism', with his lethal metaphor about facts 'killing' stories. It seems clear, indeed, from McCloskey's own words, that 'facts' have a power not attributed to the other parts of his 'tetrad', in particular, metaphors and stories, which are said only to possess the very vague power to 'criticize', with only the most nebulous indication provided of the nature, weight, and range of this 'criticism'. It might well seem that logic had the power to 'kill' a story. According to McCloskey however, 'the exact meaning of "logical" constraints on stories is elusive' (1990, p. 84). McCloskey's position regarding the relationships between the members of his tetrad remains ambiguous. One trusts, first, that he does not actually hold that the relationship between facts and stories is reciprocal, allowing well-tested facts to be 'killed' by 'good stories'. It may also be asked whether facts can 'kill' metaphors (as well as 'stories')? Does McCloskey, in fact, now accept the warning of Cristina Bicchieri? '*Pace* McCloskey no scientific metaphor persuades only because of its beauty, elegance or simplicity. If it did, one would be justified in denying its cognitive content, as generations of philosophers of science have maintained' (1988, p. 113). (Incidentally, how welcome it is to find a New Conversationalist invoking

[144]

what 'generations of philosophers of science have maintained'.)

Is it now clear, or not, that one, and perhaps two, of the components of McCloskey's new 'tetrad' wield a fundamentally different weight and authority compared with the others since well-tested facts (and perhaps logic) have the power to inflict the death sentence, or 'give life', to stories and metaphors, which do not possess any such reciprocal power, only that of some quite unspecified form of 'criticism'? Much remains uncertain and ambiguous regarding the fundamental tenets of 'the New Conversation'. For the proof of someone's methodological principles may be said to lie in their practice, and it may be noted that soon after McCloskey's insistence that well-tested facts can kill stories, we find him trying to kill well-tested facts for the sake of his own 'good' stories (see n. 4, ch. 10).

We noted above the ambivalence in *The Rhetoric of Economics* between the initial sweeping denunciations of 'The poverty of modernism', and the comforting complacency 170 pages later (see pp. 4 and 174). On this broad fundamental issue of the state of economics, six years after this somersault of 1985, McCloskey (1991b) has now performed another somersault regarding the general condition of economics. In 1985 the conclusion was that the subject was 'moderately well-off', which, in fact, was very far from being the case, as a number of more observant economists had, since 1970, already been noting (e.g. Ward, Leontief, Frisch, Phelps Brown, Gordon, Wiles, Parker, and others). Now, prompted by Klamer and Colander, McCloskey has, somewhat belatedly, recognized that something has been seriously wrong for decades, in particular with regard to the excessive and aggressive role of mathematics in economics. In 1985 McCloskey complacently suggested: 'The criticisms of economics for being "too mathematical" . . . are not very persuasive, though articulated often enough' (p. 174). Now, in 1991, McCloskey accuses economists of having 'adopted the intellectual values of the Math Department', and of having abandoned the values *methodologically* demanded by 'an empirical scientist' (1991b, pp. 8–10), which he apparently proclaims himself to be. McCloskey then argues the normatively critical, and timely *methodological* thesis that 'the procedure of modern economics is too much a search through the hyperspace of conceivable assumptions' (p. 10). 'Economic literature is largely speculative, an apparently inconclusive exploration of possible worlds' (pp. 10–11). As for Hahn's assertions regarding general equilibrium analysis, McCloskey maintains that 'his claim that GE has afforded "that precise formulation which would allow [Adam Smith's arguments] to be evaluated and their range of applicability discussed" will seem unreasonable to many economists' (p. 15). It is also noted that: 'The wholly verbal Austrian economists are as much in love with their own sort of formalism, and hostile to the notion that science might have to come off the blackboard' (p. 12). (Certainly this seems fair comment about some Austrians, such as Mises, though perhaps the distinction between 'formalism' and extreme hyper-*abstraction* may be somewhat blurred here.)

We would venture to re-emphasize that McCloskey is engaging in *methodological* criticism and problems, and in asserting a strongly normative emphasis.

He does not so much as mention the word 'rhetoric' for over three pages, and, when he does, the term is used quite harmlessly, and could easily be replaced by the recently fashionable term 'discourse', with no significant effect on the sense. (We all have our little terminological idiosyncrasies and must tolerate those of others, especially when they are so nugatory as here and part of so timely and trenchant an argument.) This is how McCloskey uses it when he does introduce the term 'rhetoric': 'The way the mathematical rhetoric has been transformed into economic rhetoric has been to *define* the economic problem as dealing with a certain kind of (easily manipulable) mathematics' (p. 9).

Sharply contrasting 'empirical work' with 'theoretical work', McCloskey maintains: 'The third rate in empirical work is still useful, something on which one can build. The third rate in theoretical work is perfectly useless, even bad for one's soul' (p. 13). He warns regarding the aims of the hyper-abstractionists and mathematicians: 'It is an open secret that they *want* economics to become a branch of the Math Department . . . . One economics department after another has been seized by the formalists and marched off to a Gulag of hyperspace searching' (p. 14).

In view of what has gone before in this note, and elsewhere, it is a pleasure to recognize Professor McCloskey's paper as a splendidly articulate, incisive, and relevant piece of *methodological* criticism. Especially welcome is McCloskey's constant, sharp emphasis on the clear distinction between the values, and the 'theoretical work' (or 'theories' or propositions), of pure mathematics, on the one hand, and

[147]

those of an empirical science, on the other. Admirably wise, also, is the appeal to some of the methods, aims, and criteria of natural sciences as highly relevant to economics. Moreover, the occasional severity of tone is amply justified on the part of an economic historian, who, like William Parker, already quoted in chapter 4, has seen the interests of his subject suffer so seriously from the aggression of mathematicians. McCloskey's paper might perhaps be criticized for the broadness of the front on which it attacks. Moreover, as suggested by another contributor to the symposium (D. W. Katzner), the target may have been somewhat misstated as consisting of 'Formalization' *as such*, rather than as formalization combined with undisciplined *hyper-abstraction*. The difficulty is that the two processes have been closely combined, because mathematical formalization has so facilitated excessive abstraction, based on vacuous, trivial, unrealistic, or ambiguous assumptions or axioms. Surely Professor Robert Solow's remark that 'rigor sometimes demands abstraction' is a serious understatement so far as economics and the social sciences are concerned. In fact, Solow's claim that 'you cannot have too much rigor' is quite unacceptable if one agrees (even if only in part) with Robert Gordon's presidential statement (1976, already quoted) that 'the mainstream of economic theory sacrifices far too much relevance in its pursuit of rigor'. As someone has observed, rigour, in economics, is a sign, too often, of the 'rigor mortis' of reality. Furthermore, Solow's statement that 'there is not a category of non-rigorous truth, not in theory' (1991, p. 31) seems to involve a misconception of the nature of 'theory' in an empirical science, and suggests that the terms 'theorems' or

[148]

'analysis' would be much more appropriate for pure mathematical 'theory'.

5. Colander states that 'Chicago is unabashedly positivist' (Klamer and Colander, 1990, p. 189). Depending on what precisely 'Chicago' means in methodological terms, this could be rather unfair to 'positivism' (though not, of course as unfair as pinning on Chicago McCloskey's usage of 'positivism' which associates 'positivists' with McCarthyism, male chauvinism, and Auschwitz). If, however, the as-if, 'let's-pretend-we-are-all-abundantly-knowledgeable' assumption is regarded as an important component of 'Chicago' methodology, then there are no grounds for describing this particular component as 'positivist'. It could be maintained that 'positivists' may, and should, agree with James Tobin that this once fashionable approach 'has done great damage' (Klamer, 1984, pp. 105–6, and ch. 5 above).

6. Just as McCloskey and Klamer stir together 'positivism' and 'modernism', so Colander seems to equate 'positivism' with 'formalism', thus rendering the vast, nebulous target of 'positivism' so comprehensive as to be difficult to miss however wild one's missile. Such a tactic is quite unnecessary for Colander who is concerned with thoroughly serious criticism. But he concludes by laying down three 'conventions', which he maintains have dominated American graduate schools since about 1950 and which he describes as 'positivist': (a) that, for students of economics, 'there is no reason to know institutions'; (b) 'that the latest literature embodies all that is worth knowing from earlier literature'; and (c) 'that one should know only the paradigm within which one works' (Klamer and Colander, 1990, p. 194).

[149]

There is not, of course, a scintilla of historical justification for describing those who support these restrictive 'conventions' as 'positivists'. In fact such terminological distortion manages to turn history upside down, because it was Auguste Comte, the founder of positivism, who vigorously criticized the more 'formalist' (e.g. Ricardian) branch of classical political economy as too narrow, and called for a much broader, sociological approach. As already noted, however, at the last moment, Colander seems to realize that something is incongruous in his terminology and he switches from 'positivism' to 'formalism', for the purposes of a series of historical contrasts. These contrasts are between Smith, the German Historicals, and Marshall on the one side, and, on the other side, Ricardo, Léon Walras and Samuelson. Smith, the German Historicals, and Marshall are described as 'sociological' (which would probably not have pleased Marshall), while Ricardo, Walras, and Samuelson are now described not as 'positivists', but by the term 'formalist' (introduced by Benjamin Ward in 1972). Perhaps Colander realized how bizarre it would have been to describe Ricardo as a 'positivist', writing decades before the founder of positivism, Auguste Comte, whose main concern in criticizing political economy was to attack precisely the narrower, 'formalist', Ricardian approach to political economy.

In fact, while to apply the term 'positivist' to any group of economists (as Marxists do to the neoclassicals) is obviously profoundly misleading, to seek to describe individual economists as 'positivists' seems usually to be even more confusing. For example, was Lionel Robbins a 'positivist'? If forthright support for the normative–positive distinction, and, in particular, the application of this distinction to the question of interpersonal comparisons of utility, are the decisive hallmarks of a 'positivist', then no one could have shown himself a more thorough-going 'positivist' than Robbins, who would, however, with his Austrian inclinations, justifiably have rejected such a description. The issue has been debated to and fro, with Cooter and Rappoport maintaining that Robbins 'embraced the positivist conception of method' (1984, pp. 523, 528), and Hennipman rejecting such a description as 'a baffling idea' (1988, p. 84). Also with regard to Milton Friedman: in spite of his famous proclamation of his allegiance to 'positive economics', that he is, or was ever, a 'positivist', in any precise or valid sense of the term, may seem doubtful (see preceding note 5).

Even as regards philosophers the term 'positivist' is pretty difficult to pin on living individuals. It is over half a century since the Vienna Circle called themselves 'logical positivists' (as distinct from 'positivists' *tout simple*) and with the assassination of Moritz Schlick, and the Nazi take-over of Austria in 1938, the group dispersed physically, and to an increasing extent intellectually. As to whether Sir Karl Popper might be called a 'positivist', he claims, personally, to have 'killed Logical Positivism' (1982, pp. 87–90). Some observers, however, might regard his doctrines of falsifiability and falsification as inclining towards some form of 'positivism'; while his *Logik der Forschung* (1934) first appeared in the Vienna Circle's series of monographs. Sometimes those proclaiming 'the death of positivism' seem to be referring simply to the short-lived Vienna Circle of 'logical positivists', while sometimes they seem to be including the much wider 'positivist' movement dating back to the middle of the nineteenth century, or earlier.

Chapter 8 Distinctions, Demarcations and Clarity

1. According to Klamer and Colander (1990, p. 8), there has been, in the USA, an increase from 15 economic journals in 1920, to 112 in 1963, to well over 200 in 1980.
2. The phrase 'anything goes' was mainly associated with Professor Paul Feyerabend, who (seemingly with approbation ascribed this doctrine to Lakatos; v. Paul Feyerabends' paper of 1970, p. 229). Recently, however, Feyerabend has stressed the differences between the sciences, emphasizing that 'the events and results that constitute the sciences have no common structure' (1987, p. 281); and he expresses a vigorous contempt for statements by philosophers about the methods of widely differing sciences, even suggesting that 'philosophy as a special subject with methods and a subject-matter of its own is on the way out' (1987, p. 119n.). So the name of Feyerabend has had to be dropped from the name-dropping.

Feyerabend also calls for a return to the doctrines, or approaches, of Mach, Einstein, and Wittgenstein. I might, perhaps, venture to add that a quotation from each of these masters, plus one from Popper, in my juvenile work of 1938, might be said to have summarized the main argument thereof, the 'Introduction' to which stated: 'The discussion of "methodological" questions – for the scientist at any rate – only has sense in connection with the practical problems of science' (Hutchison, 1938, p. 17). The point is made more lucidly and much more authoritatively by Ravetz in a passage I quoted more recently: 'The world of science is a very variegated one ... and the "methods" of science are a very heterogeneous collection of things' (Ravetz, 1971, pp. 173, 410; quoted by Hutchison, 1977, p. 36). 'Positivists', moreover, are constantly attacked by 'New Conversationalists' and others, for claiming 'certainty', necessity, and absoluteness for the methodological criteria which they propose. Regarding, however, the criteria proposed in my work of 1938, it was concluded that my book was 'not concerned to urge or to appear to urge any ultimate "necessity" or "absoluteness" about these criteria' (1938, p. 18). Just previously, it had also been emphasized that 'we are not attempting here to exalt "scientific" propositions or problems above "nonscientific" ones' (p. 12).

3. As Professor Stanley Fish has explained: 'It depends on the job you want to get done, it depends, as Richard Rorty would say, on what you want. And when you know what you want ... then you also know which arguments are better than others' (1988, pp. 23–4). Of course the question as to 'which arguments are better than others' will, or may, seem extremely different whether, on the one hand, one is simply carrying on 'a new conversation', with no clearly defined or discernible objectives (apart from the amusement or self-promotion of the 'conversationalists') or, on the other hand, if one has the objective, ultimate or proximate, of discovering, or making more accurate, economic knowledge and techniques which will render economic policies,

public or private, less unsuccessful. In other words, as Fish insists: from the New Conversationalist claims that all conversations are rhetorical and that, with the 'death' of 'positivism', 'certainty' was gone. 'Nothing follows.'

4. At this point, belatedly but none the less enthusiastically, I would like to express my far-reaching agreement with Professor Alexander Rosenberg's masterly paper: 'Economics is too important to be left to the rhetoricians' (1988a). His opening remarks on the less than serious nature of much recent 'discourse' on the methodology, or anti-methodology, of economics are especially refreshing and forthright:

> Fiddling while Rome burns. This is the impression that recent work in the methodology of economics must give. Most writers begin with an expression of relief that bad old authoritarian Logical Positivism is now dead, many go on to embrace a conventional interpretation of the moral of Kuhn's *Structure of Scientific Revolutions* [despite his own repudiation of this convenient fiction . . .], and a few gleefully embrace sophistry as a methodology of social science. All this despite the need, growing more pressing daily, for a body of knowledge about human behavior and social institutions that will enable us to improve the human condition or at least prevent its deterioration (p. 129).

From the outset Rosenberg puts vital emphasis on what was the main aim and objective of economists from Petty to Keynes:

> Of all the social sciences economics is the one to which we look most immediately for policy implications, it is the one whose form and avowed methods seem least in need of some anti-Positivist rational-

[154]

ization . . . . Moreover, even if Positivist methods were difficult to implement in full, at least they held in proper esteem the role of observational testing in the certification of knowledge: a role which no discipline that claimed the attention of policy-makers, public and private, could openly afford to degrade (p. 131).

Special attention may be called to Rosenberg's rejection of McCloskey's claim that positivism had made economists 'prone now to fanaticism and intolerance' (1985, p. 4). As Rosenberg argues:

Whether economists are fanatical or intolerant, the fault cannot be laid at the door of Positivism. For the doctrine brought to America by socialists escaping Nazism, and democrats escaping Soviet totalitarianism, was designed to combat fanaticism and intolerance. It was the Positivists' chief aim to do this by substituting experience for oracular authority in the certification of knowledge and by undercutting claims of moral certainty that breed intolerance of moral differences' (1988a, p. 133).

McCloskey's answer to Rosenberg's explanation took the form of a Socratic dialogue, with the amusing but unusual feature that Socrates-McCloskey treats his critic as a bumbling stooge to be fed lines which leave him wide open to Socratean-McCloskeyan (S-M) counter-punches (which nevertheless may land well below the belt). S-M refers, for example, to 'Hutchison's notion' of 'an authoritarian and intolerant positivism'. This is obviously an absurd distortion, as Rosenberg's admirably accurate account had made clear; and as can be easily confirmed by anyone who cares to glance at Hutchison (1938, pp. 12–18, and/or at 1941, p. 741) where may be found un-dogmatic proposals for what Colander now describes as 'reasonable conventions that are most likely to limit subjectivity and bias' (v. above, p. 56).

Chapter 9 The Non-academic Majority and Prediction: its Primary Task

1. One may venture to agree with Professor Robert Solow who 'would argue that anyone who under-stands the contents of a standard "macro" text, and has a grasp of the main economic magnitudes and the reliable economic parameters, knows vastly more than anyone who doesn't' (1989, p. 37). (One as-sumes, of course, that a non-sectarian 'macro' text for undergraduates, or first-year graduates, is being referred to.) Solow goes on to estimate that someone so equipped knows two-thirds of what is knowable at this moment, though only one-sixth of 'what one would like to know'. Two-thirds of what is knowable at the moment seems, relatively, a lot of knowledge to acquire in two or three years, and it is reasonable to assume that though this quantum of knowledge will not enable one to make a fast buck or a quick killing on the stock exchange, it probably contains quite a lot that will equip people quite often to re-duce the inaccuracy of economic predictions, at least usefully, and, in some cases, sufficiently to mitigate or ward off what (without such knowledge) might have sometimes become serious private or social catastrophes.

2. Let us again emphasize that we are only concerned with orders of magnitude. Of the Klamer/Colander

grand total of $c.130,000$ American economists in 1987, $c.77,500$ had degrees in the subject, $c.17,500$ of whom had Ph.Ds and the other $c.60,000$ MAs or below. This left $c.52,500$ without degrees, almost all of whom were working as business or government economists. Assuming a rapid rate of growth, these figures fit, very roughly indeed, with another estimate of Bellinger and Bergsten (1990, p. 701n.) for 1984, which starts from a total of 60,000 economists with degrees in the subject: of whom 38,000 were employed 'outside university and college teaching', three-fifths of whom (22,800) were in the private sector, while the other 15,200 were in government of one level or another. 'Academic' economists were estimated at 22,000. It may be of interest to compare these estimates of the numbers of economists in the USA in the mid-1980s with the figures for the UK in 1911, when that country might still, perhaps, have been considered the most important economic power in the world. According to Sir Alec Cairncross: 'In 1911 practically no government department had ever knowingly hired a professional economist . . . neither Hawtrey nor Keynes ever sat a university examination in the subject' (which President Ronald Reagan regarded as something of a disqualification). Cairncross continues: 'The same absence of demand was apparent in business' (1986, pp. 23–4).

3. On the theme of 'economics and business' Professor John Kay complains: 'If you ask most businessmen what they think economics is about, their answer will be economic forecasting. They do not think very much of economic forecasting – although they go on thinking they need it – and so they do not think very much of economists' (1991, p. 57). Kay seems to

suggest that this overriding interest of businessmen in forecasting is somehow misguided, and that they should turn their attention to recent developments in micro-economics. When Kay goes on to express the usual high hopes for novelties in economic theorizing, he does not make it clear whether the new developments in micro-economics will assist or improve predictions and forecasts. Possibly such assistance or improvement will actually emerge. Unless, however, the 'quite different, and much wider, range of policy applications' predicted by Kay as forthcoming from the new micro-economics, supply, or contribute significantly to, useful real-world forecasting or predictions, the scepticism of businessmen about economics will continue to possess much justification. Sometimes an attempt is made to distinguish between 'prediction' and 'forecasting', according to whether the underlying 'theory' is more or less explicitly formulated, and to how quantitative, or merely qualitative, the prediction may be. Practically speaking, however, this distinction has little significance (see Hutchison, 1977, pp. 12ff.).

Chapter 10   To Predict or not to Predict? (That *is* the Question)

1. For an earlier version of my views, 'On prediction and economic knowledge', see Hutchison (1977, pp. 8–33).
2. J. E. Cairnes, sometimes described as 'the last of the classical economists', and a major exponent of classical methodology, also made confident claims regarding prediction in political economy:

The announcement that free trade would enrich a country, like the announcement that water would ascend in the exhausted tube of a pump, formed a distinct prediction – a prediction that certain effects would follow from certain causes: and a prediction which wherever the experiment has been tried has been verified in the event. It is clear, therefore, that, to this extent, Political Economy lays claim, and not without valid grounds, to the power of prediction (1873, p. 303; quoted by Deane, n.d., p. 9).

3. The total 'bowdlerization' of Ricardo has already been carried out with great thoroughness by Professor Samuel Hollander, who writes: 'G. L. S. Shackle urged that a theory ought to be "a classificatory one, putting situations in this box or that according to what *can happen* as a sequel to it. Theories which tell us what *will* happen are claiming too much." This position, I maintain, was precisely that of Ricardo.' Shackle's and Hollander's concept of economic 'theory' is that of empirically and predictively vacuous taxonomy and tautology (which we have noticed Hicks included as part of economic 'theory'). To ascribe this contemporary sceptical view of economic theory to Ricardo is biographically fantastic. In fact it would be difficult to think of two writers further apart than Ricardo and Shackle on fundamental issues of the methodology of economics. It is incredible that Ricardo would ever have spent the time, effort, and money involved in buying a seat in the House of Commons and occupying it for four and a half years (or that James Mill would have been so persistently eager to put his pupil into Parliament) if all that Ricardo was concerned to deliver to his fellow MPs were taxonomic exercises of a classificatory nature, putting hypothetical situations

in this box or that (Hutchison, 1985, p. 338; Hollander, 1979, p. 640).

4. The (or a) theme of '*If You're So Smart*' (1990) is that it is fraudulent and disastrous for academic economists to offer investment advice because they are unable to make sufficiently relevant and precise predictions. This might, up to a point, be a plausible hypothesis, but well-tested facts are needed as support. Obviously, it would constitute a very good story indeed if it could be claimed that the two leading economists of their generations, Maynard Keynes in the UK, and Irving Fisher in the USA, were disastrous investors, not only in respect of their own personal investments, but on behalf of, or in their advice to, their college or university. So McCloskey writes: 'From John Maynard Keynes (who lost money regularly before breakfast, but had a Cambridge college backing him up) and Irving Fisher (who reduced Yale's endowment to half Harvard's by touting stocks in 1928) . . . , economists have not earned the confidence of bankers' (1990, p. 118).

Regarding the Keynes component of McCloskey's story, it may be said at once that it is wildly untrue. Especially objectionable is the vague insinuation that Keynes may not have kept his personal financial dealings separate from his activities as Bursar of King's. McCloskey's story about Keynes can quite easily be tested from easily obtainable, public sources, the facts being that, after some early ups and downs, he made a handsome fortune and died a very wealthy man, having served his college most successfully as Bursar, and having been made a Director of the Bank of England (on Keynes's financial activities, see *Collected Writings*, vol. XII, 1983). The Fisher component of McCloskey's story is much more complex and cannot so easily be tested against public sources. (I happen, however, to be exceptionally well placed to come to a fairly, or relatively well-informed view, living just round the corner from a former Treasurer of Yale, while my wife's former teacher is the historian of Yale, and one of her closest friends is related to the Fisher family.) It is well known – from the biography by his son – that Fisher, like countless others only more so, lost vast sums of his own money by unsuccessful investments after 1928. But this is not nearly enough for McCloskey, who wants the much better story that Fisher was responsible for vast losses by his university. Two formidable and possibly fatal objections arise regarding the Fisher component of McCloskey's story: (a) that it is very unlikely that Fisher had any influence on Yale's investment policies at this time; and (b) little or no sense can be made of McCloskey's accusation that Yale's endowment was reduced to half Harvard's.

Regarding (a), Fisher seems to have had little or no influence on the affairs of Yale, financial or otherwise, during the 1920s. He was only teaching half-time for much of the period and was much too busy with his commitments and crusades regarding teetotalism, anti-smoking, the League of Nations, the compensated dollar, etc. He seems to have been no more likely to have influenced Yale's investments than to have influenced Yale in favour of teetotalism.

As regards (b): Even if Fisher did influence Yale's investments, it makes little or no sense to accuse him, or anyone else, of having reduced Yale's endowment to half Harvard's, because from the later decades of the nineteenth century until the Second World War,

Yale's finances were regularly on a much smaller scale than Harvard's, with Yale's expenditure for many decades averaging little more than half Harvard's. As the case stands, the Fisher component of McCloskey's story can be awarded scarcely more credibility than the Keynes component. It still remains, however, quite conceivable that some solid evidence for the Fisher component of McCloskey's story might be discovered. If so, the quite plausible conclusion might emerge that not all 'good stories' told by New Conversationalists can immediately be 'killed' by well-tested facts. Nevertheless, it seems that, among the NCs, when push comes to shove, as between 'a good story' and well-tested facts, it is a 50–50 toss-up which 'kills' which. For McCloskey's support for the principle of facts testing (and even 'killing') stories is equivocal. He does not himself argue or urge that 'great emphasis' be put on this principle. He merely concedes that 'no one could object', if (for example) one were to suggest that his story about Keynes regularly losing money before breakfast should be tested against facts. This is very generous of McCloskey; but it still leaves his position fundamentally ambiguous and incoherent. (I am most grateful to Professor George W. Pierson, Professor John Perry Miller, and Mr John Ecklund for information regarding Irving Fisher and Yale.)

5. Professor McCloskey sneers just as contemptuously at political predictions as he does at economic predictions, and misunderstands and misrepresents the facts and questions just as comprehensively. He denies that political prediction can earn a profit: 'If your Truth is so valuable, why does it not meet a market test?' (1990, p. 124). The fact is that, like economic

prediction, political prediction, in the form of political risk analysis, is meeting market tests quite handsomely. Recently, as a result of important changes in political conditions and world trade patterns, as Robert Schulman explains: 'New markets have been created while existing business ventures have been shaken. Eager to get their bearings, American companies have been turning with increasing frequency to consultants who assess the potential risks and rewards abroad by analyzing the political, social and economic conditions of a particular country or region' (1990, p. 12). Specially valuable may be warnings about dangerously wasteful investments: 'American business, for example, has a nearly limitless capacity for self-delusion in regarding the Soviet Union and China as places to make large amounts of money' (has warned the analyst Richard V. Allen). Of course, the business of political risk analysis and prediction has its successes and failures: 'The business is not immune to hucksterism' (which is?). In May 1990 one firm apparently proclaimed regarding the political future of Kuwait: 'Outright invasion by either Iraq or Iran is possible but not likely.' As regards profitability, one firm is said to charge $2,500 a day, plus expenses, for work by one of its experts: while 'if you are more interested in the global outlook several years down the line', the advice and predictions of Henry Kissinger Associates are apparently available for $200,000 (which will get you 'at least one meeting' with H. K. himself). Far from political prediction not being profitable, Robert Schulman maintains: 'Judging by the number of crises in the world lately, profits must be soaring in the political risk business' (p. 12). Following the lines of his book, McCloskey may, of course, seek to defend his misplaced scepticism by overturning in this case the general Chicago 'rationality' postulate, with the charge that what is being bought and sold in this market is 'magic', or 'snake oil', etc. (1990, *passim*).

6. Already in the 1920s – between the First World War and the great slump – Pigou looked back (1929, p. 21) rather nostalgically to the 'stable general culture' in the leading European countries, amid which, in the nineteenth century, economic development had proceeded. This stable general culture was more or less implicitly and justifiably assumed by most classical and the earlier neo-classical economists, and contributed incalculably to economic stability and predictability. As a part of this stable general culture, J. S. Mill could assume, for example, that war was now banished to the remoter backward confines of the world, with minimal repercussions on more developed economies. Mill could also assume that generally a stationary state, with no net changes in population, technology, and capital stock, etc., was only 'a hand's breadth away'. Obviously, in a near-stationary state economic events and developments would be much less unpredictable. Major external shocks would come simply or mainly from the weather and natural disasters. For most of the twentieth century, stationary models, which exclude important shocks from war, political upheaval, and major technological change, could not be regarded as the reasonably close 'first approximations' which they often seemed in the nineteenth century to many classicals and neo-classicals. Consequently, the assumption, pervading so much classical and neo-classical theorizing, of widespread predictability, has

[164]

been far more unrealistic in the twentieth century,
except that, to some slight but significant extent,
gradual advances in economic predictive capacity may
have countered the forces making for increasing instability and unpredictability.

7. Professor Samuelson (3 November 1980) has expressed much more optimism than Clower: 'Economists forecast better than they did. They forecast
better than chance, better than naïve rules like "Same
tomorrow as today", better than non-economists can
do, whether they be astrologer, banker or candidate
for public office' (1983, p. 97). Samuelson recognized
that 'accurate data, promptly available on a broad
sector of the economy, are indeed a post-World War
II development' (p. 96). He feared, however, that
'although forecasting has improved, we may be
reaching a plateau. An *indeterminacy principle*
seems to dog us, beyond which we cannot penetrate'
(pp. 97–8). Samuelson provided a valuable and authoritative corrective to the more unreasonable kinds
of pessimism, though it may be difficult to share all
of his optimism. For the 'plateau' he discussed might
turn out to be something of a decline, because of
institutional changes making for greater instability and
unpredictability. Such increasing instability would not,
however, diminish the value of the predictive contribution of economists, provided this contribution
could continue, on the average, to produce less inaccurate predictions or forecasts than would be
forthcoming without the efforts of economists – and
provided also, of course, that business and government are not discouraged from making the necessary
resources available for less inaccurate predictions by
misconceived or ill-informed scepticism which quite

[165]

irrelevantly demands that economic predictions achieve the very high standard of precision and probability attained by some of the natural sciences.

8. Alexander Rosenberg's emphasis on the demand for predictions from both private enterprise and government is very timely. Though it ought to be unnecessary to stress the position of economics as a, or the, leading policy science, Rosenberg's insistence is well justified: 'While science may or may not require prediction, *we do*. It is a large part of what we look to science for. It is what we need to ameliorate the human condition' (1988a, p. 147). Quoting Roy Weintraub, Rosenberg observes that the market pays for the predictions of economists, 'not because it deems them entertaining, but because it deems them reliable, or at least more reliable than other predictions' (1987, p. 143) – which rightly and totally contradicts McCloskey's views. Rosenberg concludes: 'McCloskey seems pretty completely committed to a policy-irrelevant economics' (1988a, p. 147). This conclusion may seem inevitable, but was, quite predictably, contested by Socrates-McCloskey (p. 165).

9. The question has been asked by David Colander (1991, p. 19) whether a strike of economists would have any significant effects, or inflict any significant deprivation on the community. Colander seems inclined to answer in the negative. A valid answer obviously depends on what kind of economists went on strike. It might, perhaps, be maintained that a strike of *academic* economists would have to last a very long time for any serious effects to be felt. On the other hand, a 100 per cent effective, world-wide strike of statisticians which cut off, totally and lastingly, the supply of all economic statistics and surveys,

public and private, would probably in a few weeks, certainly in a few months, create vast problems for most kinds of major economic decision-making, public and private, with very disturbing, or even chaotic consequences. Certainly, 200–300 years ago, with considerable economic progress going forward, decision-makers had to make do with very little in the way of statistics. Economic life, however, was then on a far smaller scale compared with the late twentieth century. Decisions had to be, and were, often not too unsuccessfully, taken on the impressionistic observation of local conditions. In the limiting case, Robinson Crusoe did not need statistics, though a diary would have been helpful. Degrees of economic instability and insecurity, moreover, were, or had to be, tolerated which might soon today lead to chaos, or something like it. What sort of 'rational expectations' could be formed in large or world markets with no economic or financial statistics on which to base them?

Chapter 11 Postscript

1. In 1984, on grounds of academic freedom, I was prepared to defend games-playing in economics, or 'economics for pleasure' (Shackle) or 'beauty'. For this, however, I was rebuked, later in the same volume, by Professor Peter Wiles, who argued:

> I deny, then, the 'strong grounds in academic freedom for protecting serious academic interests which may, like pure mathematics, have no relevance or relation to any kind of real-world fruitfulness or policy making' that lead Hutchison (chapter 1, p. 14) to

allow scientists to play around without even the hope of a (1) serious or (2) useful outcome. I am saying *as a taxpayer* that the public funding of science should be more sceptical and more Philistine. What people do after hours with their already earned income is their own affair – and the recognition of *that* sufficiently preserves academic freedom. Freedom is the absence of human restraints, not the presence of state subsidies (Wiles, 1984, pp. 312–13).

Since 1984, in the case of economics, I have, somewhat reluctantly, become much inclined to accept Wiles's strictures, because it seems that a statement such as the following, even if it is considerably exaggerated, and based mainly, or entirely, on American experience, contains a disquieting amount of truth:

When one uses economic analysis to study the economics profession, what one sees is not very pretty. What one sees is the following: Academic economists, following their own self-interest, have diverted economic analysis from looking at real issues to playing mind-games that are fun for academic economists but of little use for society. Academic economists are allowed to continue these mind-games because what they do is not subject to the test of the market. What's happened in the economics profession is a wonderful example of what economic reasoning says will happen to any group in society that is not subject to market forces (Colander, 1991, p. 4).

2. A grim example of the transformation of a serious subject into a nihilistic academic game is provided by the fate, in recent decades, of Literary Criticism. See the impressive account in David Lehman, 1991.

[168]

Bibliography

Allen, W. R. 1974: Economics, economists and economic policy: modern American experiences. Paper to the Copenhagen Conference of the Economic History Society.

Backhouse, R. E. 1991a; Mathematics and the axiomatization of general equilibrium theory. Discussion paper, Economics Dept, University of Birmingham.

Backhouse, R. E. 1991b: Rhetoric and methodology. Discussion paper, Economics Dept, University of Birmingham.

Balabkins, N. W. 1988: *Not by Theory alone*.

Baumol, W. J. 1991: Towards a newer economics. *Economic Journal*, 101, 1ff.

Bellinger, W. K. and Bergsten, G. S 1990: The market for economic thought. *History of Political Economy*, 22, 1697ff.

Bicchieri, C. 1988: Should a scientist abstain from metaphor? In A. Klamer, D. McCloskey and R. Solow (eds), *The Consequences of Economic Rhetoric*, 100ff.

[169]

Blaug, M. 1988: John Hicks and the methodology of economics. In N. de Marchi (ed.), *The Popperian Legacy in Economics*, 183ff.

Bloom, A. 1987: *The Closing of the American Mind.*

Bombach, G., Ramser, H. J. and Timmermann, M. (eds) 1976: *Der Keynesianismus*, 2 vols.

Buchholz, T. G. 1990: *New Ideas from Old Economists.*

Cairncross, Sir Alec 1986: *Economics and Economic Policy.*

Cairnes, J. E. 1873: *Essays in Political Economy.*

Clark, J. B. 1899: *The Distribution of Wealth.*

Clower, R. 1964: Monetary history and positive economics. *Journal of Economic History*, 24, 364ff.

Clower, R. 1989: The state of economics: hopeless but not serious. In A. W. Coats and D. C. Colander (eds), *The Spread of Economic Ideas*, 23ff.

Coase, R. H. 1975: Marshall on method. *Journal of Law and Economics*, 18, 25ff.

Coase, R. H. 1988: *The Firm, the Law and the Market.*

Coats, A. W. 1991: What Mirowski's history leaves out. (typescript review)

Colander, D. 1989: The invisible hand of truth. In A. W. Coats and D. C. Colander (eds), *The Spread of Economic Ideas*, 31ff.

Colander, D. C. 1991: *Why aren't Economists as Important as Garbagemen?*

Cooter, R. and Rappoport, P. 1984: Were the ordinalists wrong about welfare economics? *Journal of Economic Literature*, XXII, 507ff.

Deane, P. n.d.: An accurate, clear-headed Cambridge man: J. N. Keynes and the new economic science. (typescript)

Debreu, G. 1959: *The Theory of Value.*

Debreu, G. 1991: The mathematization of economic theory. *American Economic Review*, 81(1), 1ff.

Devons, E. 1961: *Essays in Economics.*

Economist 1987: Book review, 7 February, 96ff.

Edgeworth, F. Y. 1897: The pure theory of monopoly. In *Papers Relating to Political Economy*, vol. 1, 111ff.

Feyerabend, P. 1970: Consolations for the specialist. In I. Lakatos and A. Musgrave (eds), *Criticism and the Growth of Knowledge*, 197ff.

Feyerabend, P. 1987: *Farewell to Reason.*

Fish, S. 1980: *Is There a Text in this Class?*

Fish, S. 1988: Comments from outside economics. In A. Klamer, D. McCloskey and R. Solow (eds), *The Consequences of Economic Rhetoric*, 21ff.

Friedman, M., 1991: Old wine in new bottles. *Economic Journal*, 101, 33ff.

Frisch, R. 1970: Econometrics in the world today. In *Induction, Growth and Trade: Essays in Honour of Sir Roy Harrod*, 162–3.

Gårdlund, T. 1958: *Life of Knut Wicksell.*

Goodwin, C. 1989: Doing good and spreading the gospel. In A. W. Coats and D. C. Colander (eds), *The Spread of Economic Ideas*, 157ff.

Gordon, R. A. 1976: Rigor and relevance in a changing institutional setting. *American Economic Review*, LXVI, 1ff.

Grubel, H. and Boland, L. A. 1986: On the efficient use of mathematics in economics. *Kyklos*, 39, 419ff.

Hahn, F. H. 1970: Some adjustment problems. *Econometrica*, 38, 1ff.

Hahn, F. H. 1973: *On the Notion of Equilibrium in Economics.*

Hahn, F. H. 1984: *Equilibrium and Macroeconomics.*

Hahn, F. H. 1990: John Hicks, the theorist. *Economic Journal*, 100, 539ff.

Hahn, F. H. 1991: The next hundred years. *Economic Journal*, 101, 47ff.

Hall, Sir R. 1959: Reflections on the practical application of economics. *Economic Journal*, 69, 659ff.

Hardach, K. 1980: *The Political Economy of Germany in the Twentieth Century.*

Hayek, F. A. 1933: *Monetary Theory and the Trade Cycle.*

Hayek, F. A. 1939: *Profits, Interest and Investment.*

Hayek, F. A. 1960: *The Constitution of Liberty.*

Hayek, F. A. 1988: *The Fatal Conceit.*

Hennipman, P. 1988: A new look a the ordinalist revolution. *Journal of Economic Literature*, XXVI, 80ff.

Hicks, Sir John 1946: *Value and Capital*, 2nd edn.

Hicks, Sir John 1963: *Theory of Wages*, 2nd edn.

Hicks, Sir John 1965: *Capital and Growth.*

Hicks, Sir John 1979: *Causation in Economics.*

Hicks, Sir John 1983: *Classics and Moderns.*

Hollander, S. 1979: *The Economics of David Ricardo.*

Hollis, M. and Nell, E. J. 1975: *Rational Economic Man.*

Hoover, K. D. 1991: Mirowski's screed. *Methodus*, 3(1), 139ff.

Hutchison, T. W. 1938: *The Significance and Basic Postulates of Economic Theory.*

Hutchison, T. W. 1941: The significance and basic postulates of economic theory: a reply to Professor Knight. *Journal of Political Economy*, XLIX, 732ff.

Hutchison, T. W. 1953: *A Review of Economic Doctrines, 1870–1929.*

Hutchison, T. W. 1968: *Economists and Economic Policy in Britain , 1946–1966.*

Hutchison, T. W. 1977: *Knowledge and Ignorance in Economics.*

Hutchison, T. W. 1978: *Revolutions and Progress in Economic Knowledge.*

Hutchison, T. W. 1981: On the aims and methods of economic theorizing. Ch. 9 in *The Politics and Philosophy of Economics,* 266ff.

Hutchison, T. W. 1985: On the interpretation and misinterpretation of economists. In P. Roggi (ed.), *Gli Economistic e la politica economica,* 323ff.

Hutchison, T. W. 1986: Omniscience or omni-nescience about the future? In I. Kirzner (ed.), *Subjectivism, Intelligibility and Economic Understanding,* 122ff.

Huxley, J. Haddon, A. C. and Carr-Saunders, A. M. 1936: *We Europeans: a Study of Racial Problems.*

Jouvenel, B. de n.d.: *L'Art de la Conjecture.*

Kaldor, Lord 1960: *Essays on Value and Distribution.*

Kaldor, Lord 1972: The irrelevance of equilibrium economics. *Economic Journal,* 82, 1238.

Katzner, D. W. 1991: In defence of formalization in economics. *Methodus,* 3(1), 17ff.

Kay, J. A. 1991: Economics and business. *Economic Journal,* 101, 57ff.

Keynes, Lord 1983: *Collected Writings,* vol. 12, ed. D. Moggridge.

Klamer, A. 1984: *Conversations with Economists.*

Klamer, A. and Colander, D. 1990: The Making of an Economist. (See also *Journal of Economic Perspectives,* Fall 1987, 95ff.)

Klamer, A., McCloskey, D. and Solow, R. (eds) 1988: *The Consequences of Economic Rhetoric.*

Koertge, N. 1979: Braucht die Sozialwissenschaft wirklich Metaphysik? In H. Albert and K. H. Stapf (eds), *Theorie und Erfahrung, Beiträge zur Grundlagenproblematik der Sozialwissenschaft,* 55ff.

Komlos, J. and Landes, R. 1991: Alice to the Red Queen:

imperious econometrics. *Economic History Review*, XLIV, 133ff.

Korsch, A. 1976: Der Stand der beschäftigungspolitische Diskussion zur Zeit der Wirtschaftskrise in Deutschland. In G. Bombach, H. J. Ramser and M. Timmermann (eds), *Der Keynesianismus*, 2 vols, vol.1, 48ff.

Kuhn, T. S. 1970: *The Structure of Scientific Revolutions*, 2nd edn.

Kuttner, R. 1985: The poverty of economics. *Atlantic Monthly*, 255(2), 74ff.

Lawson, C. 1990: Undergraduate economics. *Royal Economic Society Newsletter*, 70, 24ff.

Lehman, D. 1991: *Signs of the Times*.

Leontief, W. 1971: Theoretical assumptions and unobserved facts. *American Economic Review*, LXI, 1ff.

Loasby, B. J. 1989: Frank Hahn's struggle of escape. Ch. 9 in *The Mind and Method of the Economist*, 119ff.

McCloskey, D. 1985: *Rhetoric of Economics*.

McCloskey, D. 1988: Two replies and a dialogue. *Economics and Philosophy*, 4, 156ff.

McCloskey, D. 1989a: Why I am no longer a positivist. First draft, conference paper.

McCloskey, D. 1989b: Why I am no longer a positivist. *Review of Social Economy*, XLVII, 225.

McCloskey, D. 1990: *If You're so Smart . . .*

McCloskey, D. 1991a: Conditional economic history: a reply to Komlos and Landes. *Economic History Review*, XLIV, 120ff.

McCloskey, D. 1991b: Economic science: a search through the hyperspace of assumptions? *Methodus*, 3(1), 6ff.

Marshall, A. 1961: *Principles of Economics*, 2 vols, ed. C. W. Guillebaud.

Marx, K. 1951: *Theories of Surplus Value*, tr. G. A. Bonner and E. Burns.

Mirowski, P. 1988: *Against Mechanism.*

Mirowski, P. 1989: *More Heat than Light.*

Morishima, M. 1984: The good and bad uses of mathematics. In P. Wiles and G. Routh (eds), *Economics in Disarray*, 51ff.

O'Brien, D. 1988: *Lionel Robbins.*

O'Brien, D. 1991: Theory and empirical observation. Working paper 98, Dept of Economics, University of Durham.

Oswald, A. J. 1991: Progress and micro-economic data. *Economic Journal*, 101, 75ff.

Parker, W. N. (ed.) 1986: *Economic History and the Modern Economist.*

Pen, J. 1985: *Among Economists.*

Phelps Brown, Sir H. 1972: The under-development of economics. *Economic Journal*, 82, lff.

Pigou, A. C. 1922: Empty economic boxes. *Economic Journal*, 32, 458ff.

Pigou, A. C. (ed.) 1925: *Memorials of Alfred Marshall.*

Pigou, A. C. 1929: *Economics of Welfare*, 3rd edn.

Pigou, A. C. 1939: Presidential address to the Royal Economic Society. *Economic Journal*, 49, 215ff.

Political Economy Club 1876: *Revised Report of Proceedings of May 31st, 1876.*

Popper, Sir Karl 1959: *Logic of Scientific Discovery.*

Popper, Sir Karl 1982: *Unended Quest*, rev. edn.

Ravetz, J. R. 1971: *Scientific Knowledge and its Social Problems.*

Robbins, Lord 1932/1980: *Essay on the Nature and Significance of Economic Science*, 1st and 3rd edns.

Robbins, Lord 1971: *Autobiography of an Economist.*

Robinson, J. 1932: *Economics is a Serious Subject.*

Robinson, J. 1933: *Economics of Imperfect Competition.*

Robinson, J. 1965: *Collected Economic Papers*, vol. 3.

[175]

Robinson, J. and Eatwell, J. 1973: *An Introduction to Modern Economics.*

Rosenberg, A. 1987: Weintraub's aim. *Economics and Philosophy,* 3(1), 143ff.

Rosenberg, A. 1988a: Economics is too important to be left to the rhetoricians. *Economics and Philosophy,* 4(1), 129ff.

Rosenberg, A. 1988b: Rhetoric is not important enough for economists to bother about. *Economics and Philosophy,* 4(1), 173ff.

Rotwein, E. 1979: The Methodological Basis of Institutional Economics. *Journal of Economic Issues,* 13–4, 1031ff.

Rotwein, E. 1983: Flirting with a priorism. *History of Political Economy,* 15, 669ff.

Samuelson, P. 1983: *Economics from the Heart,* ed. M. C. Keating.

Schlick, M. 1925/1974: *Allgemeine Erkenntnislehre.* (Eng. tr. 1974)

Schulman, R. 1990: A world in flux means steady work for risk analysts. *New York Times Business Supplement,* 4 Nov., 12ff.

Senior, N. W. 1827: *Introductory Lecture.*

Senior, N. W. 1878: *Conversations with M. Thiers, M. Guizot and others.*

Shackle, G. L. S. 1972: *Epistemics and Economics.*

Simon, H. 1976: From substantive to procedural rationality. In S. J. Latsis (ed.), *Method and Appraisal in Economics,* 129ff.

Sloane, P. J. 1990: Symposium on the market for economists in the U. K. *Royal Economic Society Newsletter,* 69, 19ff.

Solow, R. 1989: Faith, hope and charity; and How economic ideas turn to mush. In A. W. Coats and D. C.

Colander (eds), *The Spread of Economic Ideas*, 37ff. and 78ff.

Solow, R. 1991: Discussion notes on 'formalization'. *Methodus*, 31(1), 30ff.

Stolper, F. 1967: *The German Economy from 1870 to the Present Day*.

Tawney, R. H. 1952: *Equality*.

Temin, p. 1989: *Lessons from the Great Depression*.

Towse, R. and Blaug, M. 1988: *The Current State of the Economics Profession*. Royal Economic Society.

Tullock, G. 1989: Changing incentives to make economics more realistic. In A. W. Coats and D. C. Colander (eds). *The Spread of Economic Ideas*, 235ff.

Van Dyke, D. T. 1986: How to measure the performance of a business economics unit. *Business Economics*, April, 21ff.

Varian, H. 1991: Review of Mirowski, P., *More Heat than Light. Journal of Economic Literature*, XXIX(2), 595.

Walker, D. A. 1991: *Economics as social physics. Economic Journal*, 101, 615ff.

Walras, L. 1989/1936: *Economie politique appliquée*.

Ward, B. 1972: *What's Wrong with Economics?*

Weintraub, E. R. 1989: Methodology doesn't matter, but the history of economic thought might. *Scandinavian Journal of Economics*, 91(2), 477ff.

Weintraub, E. R. 1991: *Stabilizing Dynamics*.

Wiles, P. and Routh, G. (eds) 1984: *Economics in Disarray*.

Worswick, G. D. N. 1972: Is progress in economic science possible? *Economic Journal*, 82, 75ff.

Index of Names

Index of Subjects

abstraction
  Frisch, Leontief and
    Worswick on, 18–19
  and formalism, 29,
    148
  Morishima on, 113
  and the 'optimistic'
    method, 35–6, 119
  Ricardo and, 104
  and rigor, 114, 148
academic freedom, 167
aims of economists
  Edgeworth and, 93
  Marshall and, 6–7, 106
  neo-classicals and,
    6–10
  Petty and, 1–3
  Pigou and, 94
  Rosenberg on, 154–5
  Schmoller and, 8

American leadership, 32,
  39
assumptions fundamental,
  94, 131
  and realism of, 36–7,
    149
Austrian economists
  and great depression,
    109–10, 112–13
  McCloskey on, 146
  and prediction, 78

Britain, economics in,
  115–17
British tradition in
  economics, 40–1
business cycle, 9–10

Chicago, and 'positivism,'
  149

[183]